DAN WALKER'S FOOTBALL THRONKERSAURUS

WITH GERSHON PORTNOI

**SIMON &
SCHUSTER**

London · New York · Sydney · Toronto · New Delhi

A CBS COMPANY

First published in Great Britain by Simon & Schuster UK Ltd, 2014
A CBS company

1 3 5 7 9 10 8 6 4 2

Simon & Schuster UK Ltd
222 Gray's Inn Road
London WC1X 8HB

www.simonandschuster.co.uk

Simon & Schuster Australia,
Sydney

Simon & Schuster India,
New Delhi

A CIP catalogue record for this book is
available from the British Library

Hardback ISBN: 978-1-47113-629-0
Ebook ISBN: 978-1-47113-630-6

Printed in Italy by L.E.G.O SpA

CONTENTS

FOREWORD

I must have been asked a hundred times to put a newly invented word in the dictionary. Each time the creator is convinced they've come up with something perfect, a word that fills a gap we didn't even know existed. And I sympathise, because I've come up with a few of my own. But, with a deep breath, I've always had to explain that it's not up to me – that it needs all of us to love the word, use it and keep using it – if it's to stand a chance of becoming 'official'. Because, although English will always be completely democratic, most of us still like to think of the dictionary as being the Collina of the word. Forget the petitions, bite back the protests – the ref's word is final. End of story.

Except it isn't, thanks to Mr Dan Walker. Sitting next to me for the first time in Dictionary Corner, he took precisely three minutes to describe, define and illustrate the thronker. I'm not sure I've ever heard such a specific set of rules in my life – four criteria to meet before a goal even gets a look-in, 11 for the whole shebang – but I knew instantly that the thronker had legs. It's short, it's sassy, and it delivers like a slam dunk from the mouth, if you'll forgive a metaphor from the wrong sport.

A sure-fire sign of a word getting ahead is when we begin to play around with it – a sort of verbal keepy-uppy. And thronker has no limits. In a few years' time, I like to think we'll be able to thronk a mosquito as well as a ball, be thronked in Scrabble, and have a thronking good holiday. 'Thronk!' will be the new 'Kapow!' in comics, and thronkers may even become a nine-letter word on *Countdown*. The world will belong to the thronker.

And it will be richly deserved. Because you honestly won't find a nicer or brighter word inventor/broadcaster than Dan. He is also extremely funny, as you're about to find out. From now on, alongside the Panenka Penalty and the Cruyff Turn, will stand the Walker Thronk – or the Thronker Walk, one of the two.

Susie Dent

Tweed is acceptable in only two places: at Cheltenham Races and on *Countdown*

INTRODUCTION

I really hope you are currently sitting on a toilet. When I was first approached about writing this tome that is what I had in mind – somebody somewhere sitting on the throne, having a little giggle to themselves or perhaps learning something about the game of football.

That is why the last page of the book is perforated – just in case you've run out of the essentials. I'll warn you now that it is neither soft, strong or very, very long so use it only in emergencies.

My plan all along was to come up with some vaguely intelligent football guff because I know that the vast majority of you reading this know the game just as well as I do. The purpose of the book is not to educate the recently recruited fan about the vagaries of 4-2-3-1, debate the use and/or over-reliance on a 'false nine' or put right some of the sport's great wrongs. The whole idea was to come up with something that celebrates our mild obsession with football, the love of the statistic and the minutiae of the game.

I do not stand before you as a great of the game and this is by no means an autobiography detailing my 'against-all-odds' rise to the top. It's just meant to be a bit of fun that concentrates on one of the few things that unites us and brings us together no matter what language we speak – the game of football.

I also love the fact that a lot of this book – actually, the reason why it came about in the first place – is down to you. The fact that you have made #TuesdayTeamNews* such a popular part of Twitter was one of the things that initially pricked the ears of the publisher. Thousands of you send in your themed puns each week and many of them have been included here.

So when you are reading this – possibly on the toilet – you have every right to think that in some way you are responsible for what lies before you. If you will allow me to expand the argument a little further, if you dislike what you read beyond this point, you are just as much to blame as I am.

The other slightly odd thing about this book is the title. 'What exactly is a *Thronkersaurus*?' my mother asked when I told her what the title was. Well, all that is explained in the chapter called 'Thronkers', and when my evil plan comes to fruition the next generation of football fans will hopefully be using it to describe the great goals that they score and watch.

I really hope you enjoy reading it, telling your football friends about it and explaining to your football-hating comrades why it is a seminal piece of work. I shall leave you to it.

*#TuesdayTeamNews is a social media thing that happens every Tuesday at 09:31 (see pages 14–16). You can also join in each week by finding @MrDanWalker.

Every broadcast should be preceded by a deep groinal stretch

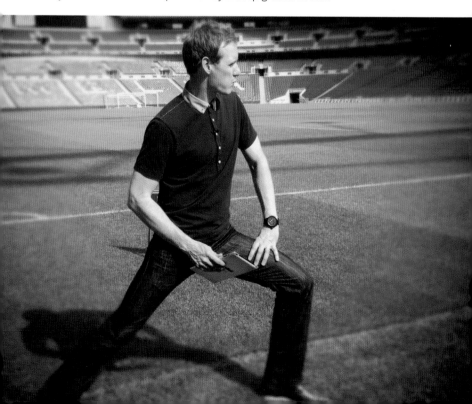

THE MOST DANGEROUS JOBS IN FOOTBALL

I love my job and, although I'm not a violent man, I'd definitely fight you for it. OK, I wouldn't punch you in the face, but I'd at least try to administer a firm headlock. My current employment feels a long way from where I started out. My first day at McDonald's didn't go quite as I'd hoped. I was late for work because it took me ages to get the trousers on! I don't know whether they mis-measured me or my rear was remarkably oversized, but they were so tight I was beginning to think a giant shoe-horn was the only way into them.

I worked as a burger-flipper for a month, but in that time the trousers continually looked like they had been sprayed on. To make matters worse, I was also given an official warning for putting too many McNuggets in my lunch allowance, and had two near-death experiences.

The first of these took place in a McDonald's massive fridge. I went in there early one morning to retrieve some shredded lettuce, but the door mechanism released and I was locked in for about two hours. There's not much you can do in a locked fridge for that length of time. I embarked on a vigorous press-up regime to keep warm and was eventually saved by a vast supply of cheese slices. I noticed there was a small gap underneath the fridge door and started pushing the slices through it to make what I can only describe as a cheese-train. A colleague eventually spotted my cheesy SOS and released me from the chilly dungeon.

We had to write it up in the accident book and we titled it 'Fridge Peril'.

The second incident was even more serious. Two days after fridgegate (no one called it that) the same thing happened in the freezer. You'd think I'd have learned my lesson but, as I wandered aimlessly into the vast frozen kingdom at the back of the McDonald's in Crawley, the door mechanism failed and I was once again locked in a very cold room. The difference here was the temperature – minus 18 is mighty chilly, especially when your only protection is a thin, striped t-shirt and those spray-on trousers. There was no gap under the door and no cheese singles. After about ten minutes in the arctic darkness I was fearing the worst. I admit that I thought I was going to die and be found among huge boxes of McNuggets and Apple Pies. Thankfully, just as my eyes were beginning to frost over, the assistant manager opened the door to count the number of burger boxes he had left... salvation!

Another entry in the accident book was required, and this time we imaginatively went for 'Freezer Peril'.

Despite my torrid time at McDonald's it remains the place where I received the most significant compliment of my working life. On the day I told the assistant boss (the same one who had rescued me from the freezer) that I was leaving to work in Dillons The Bookstore for 20p more an hour, he took me to one side and uttered the words I will never forget:

'Dan, I'll be honest with you... you just can't go... no one works the chicken-station like you.' He was right, but the world of literature was calling my name.

FOOTBALLERS' FIRST JOBS

It might not have been McDonald's, but plenty of footballers started their wage-earning careers with jobs that were less than glamorous. Here's a selection for you but, to the best of my knowledge, none of them involves potential freezing-to-death scenarios.

CHRIS WADDLE
England's finest mullet started out working in a sausage factory making seasoning for the bangers.

PETER SCHMEICHEL
The great Dane only turned pro at 24, by which time he'd been supplementing his part-time football income with carpet-fitting, newspaper ad-space selling and working as a cleaner.

ALEX FERGUSON
The Old Trafford legend served five years as an apprentice tool-maker and also had a stint as a restaurant chef before deciding to focus solely on football. Good decision.

JIMMY BULLARD

Before West Ham offered him a contract, the curly-haired midfield magician used to be a painter and decorator.

ANDY HESSENTHALER

The Gillingham cult hero started his working life as a bathroom fitter.

STUART PEARCE

Before making Pizza Hut adverts for a living, Psycho used to work part-time as an electrician and plumber while playing for non-League Wealdstone.

RICKIE LAMBERT

He's had an amazing last few seasons but during a lull in the early part of his career, the striker took a job at a beetroot factory. He was responsible for putting lids on jars of the purple stuff.

PAPISS CISSE

When the striking sensation was just 15, he used to drive an ambulance from his town in Senegal to another which had a hospital with better facilities. A sobering thought.

The Dog Ate My Homework... and other poor excuses for missing a match

I might have missed work due to being locked in a fridge and then a freezer (once was unlucky, twice careless, I know, I know) but plenty of footballing types have not shown up for work for a whole host of ludicrous reasons. Here's a selection...

Hans-Joachim Watzke

The Borussia Dortmund chairman missed the last few minutes of his club's Champions League semi-final second leg against Real Madrid in May 2013 because he locked himself in the toilet. He was unable to take the tension after the Spanish side scored two late goals to almost deny the Germans their place in the final. 'For the first time in my life I had to give up due to heart problems. I went to the toilet for the last minutes, locked myself in, covered my ears and looked at my watch. I had all kinds of thoughts going through my head.'

Santiago Canizares

The Spanish goalkeeper was preparing for a night out when he dropped a bottle of aftershave on his foot. The glass smashed, severing a tendon, which meant the goalkeeper missed the entire 2002 World Cup. On the plus side, he smelled great.

Alex Stepney

In 1975, the Manchester United goalkeeper was sidelined by a broken jaw. But it hadn't been inflicted during an aerial collision or even a fight. No, Stepney managed to dislocate his jaw by yelling too hard at his defenders during a match against Birmingham.

Darren Barnard

The Barnsley player was house-training his puppy, but not very successfully as he managed to slip in a puddle of dog wee when walking into his kitchen and tore knee ligaments.

Liam Lawrence

A pesky dog also sidelined the Stoke midfielder, who tripped over his pooch, fell down the stairs and muffed up his knee.

Milan Rapaic

The Hajduk Split player missed the start of one season due to an unusual holiday injury. Rapaic managed to poke himself in the eye with his boarding pass while in the airport, causing sufficient sight damage for a significant stint on the sidelines.

Dennis Bergkamp

At least Rapaic made it to the airport. The Arsenal striker would do no such thing given his fear of flying, which saw him miss countless Champions League away games for the Gunners.

Jerome Boateng

No fear of flying for the former Manchester City defender who was on a plane on the way back from international duty when he aggravated an existing knee injury by colliding with a drinks trolley. He was out for a month.

David James

The former England goalkeeper once lived up to his 'Calamity' nickname when he managed to pull a muscle in his back while reaching for the TV remote control at home. He needs one of those chairs with the controls in the arm.

David Batty

The no-nonsense midfielder re-injured an old Achilles tendon problem when his toddler ran him over with his tricycle. I'm not making this up. Promise.

Alan Wright

The tiny full-back strained his knee while reaching for the pedal in his new Ferrari – which was quickly replaced by a Rover 416. Rumour has it his feet were a UK size 3, which is basically like a trotter.

LOCKED UP

Other footballers haven't turned up to play for a slightly less bizarre, far more simple reason: they weren't allowed to because they were in prison, detained at Her Majesty's pleasure – or at least they were at some point.

IAN WRIGHT

We've all forgotten to tax and insure our cars, right? Before he turned pro, Wrighty forgot to pay his dues for both of his motors and was subsequently handed a 14-day prison sentence for his amnesia.

STIG TOFTING

Bolton's Danish midfielder was out with team-mates after the 2002 World Cup when he managed to head-butt a Copenhagen restaurant owner. He was eventually sentenced to four months in prison, causing him to miss the end of Wanderers' 2002/03 season.

NIZAR TRABELSI

Any old footballer can get jailed for trivialities like car irregularities and common assault, but the Fortuna Dusseldorf player's charge sheet was a tad different. He was arrested after his first and only match on account of his al-Qaeda links and subsequently locked up for ten years in 2003 for plotting an attack against US soldiers stationed at a Belgian airbase.

JOEY BARTON

Mr Barton had a number of run-ins with The Fuzz before becoming a *Question Time* regular. He served 77 days for driving his car into a pedestrian in Liverpool city centre.

PETER STOREY

One double with Arsenal in 1971 was not enough for Storey, who served three years for his part in a plot to forge gold coins in 1980 and then got 28 days for illegally trying to import pornographic grot films ten years later.

MICKEY THOMAS

The Welsh former Manchester United star was convicted of counterfeiting and money laundering (with the unwitting help of the Wrexham youth team) for which he served 18 months in the nick.

DUNCAN FERGUSON

Big Dunc was sentenced to a three-month stretch back in 1994 after head-butting Raith's John McStay while playing for Rangers. Not only is that illegal in football, it's also illegal in the UK.

TONY ADAMS

Mr Arsenal was not the first footballer to receive a custodial sentence for drink-driving. But he was almost certainly the first player to be allegedly four times over the legal limit after crashing his car into a wall.

GARY CHARLES

The former England and Nottingham Forest full-back may be most famous for being on the receiving end of Gazza's rash challenge in the 1991 FA Cup final, but he was also imprisoned for drink-driving. Upon his release, he had to wear an electronic tag but he was soon back in prison after he cut it off in order to leave the country for a holiday.

GEORGE BEST

One of football's saddest tales. The tricky legend-turned-alcoholic walked something of a tightrope with the law for much of his career, but it was hitting a policeman (and drink-driving and failing to answer bail) that saw him receive a three-month sentence in 1984. He still managed to turn out for the Ford open prison football team while doing his time.

What exactly is all this Tuesday Team News business?

'I've got no idea what you're on about. It sounds like a complete pile of rubbish,' was Alan Shearer's assessment when I suggested that Alan Sheep Shearer was just not a good enough pun to make it into the Farmyard XI. I explained to the former striker that when you have players of the quality of Get Off My Landon Donovan the bar was a lot higher than normal. These weren't your average puns... these babies were top-quality efforts from full-time PUNdits.

And that is essentially the magic of Tuesday Team News. A few years ago I stumbled upon some BBC Sport colleagues during the first game of the 2010 World Cup between South Africa and Mexico. We were enjoying a bite to eat in a cafe on Long Street in Cape Town. Paul Birch and Tom McCoy are two lovely fellas who help write the stats and analysis for major football tournaments – and anything else the BBC covers. We were eating fish and some clown suggested we attempt to come up with a list of footballers with fishy names. Prawn Wright-Phillips made us chuckle as did Cod Wallace and Langoustine Babayaro. In the blink of an eye about four hours had passed.

The next day I set off on my 5,000-kilometre double-decker bus tour of South Africa and one of our first stops was Bloemfontein. I was reading a *Rough Guide* to the place where England would eventually be humbled by Germany and discovered that it was the birthplace of J.R.R. Tolkien. I took to Twitter and asked my ten thousand or so followers whether they could come up with a Lord Of The Rings XI. The time was 09:31 and the day was a Tuesday. Tuesday Team News was born and has grown from those small beginnings into an unwieldy beast that takes up far too much of my time and makes people very angry when their suggestions are not included in the final squad.

The game has one simple rule: once I announce the team theme at 09:31 each Tuesday, suggestions have to involve some sort of pun on a player's name – there must be a change. For example, Marc Overmars is dull and uncreative and would have no chance of making the Chocolate XI but Marc OverPars might squeeze on to the subs' bench for the Golf XI.

On that rather chilly morning in Bloemfontein the suggestions started coming in: Bobby Mordor for captain, Legolassana Diarra in midfield, and Pete from Ipswich demanded a place in the dugout for Gandalf Ramsey. I published the team later that day and got my first set of furious responses from people whose puns didn't quite reach the required standard.

Within a few weeks Tuesday Team News had become something of a social media fixture. I was on a tube at 09:31 one Tuesday and emerged in the sunshine at Oxford Circus with a Twitter feed full of angry 'Where is this week's theme?' messages. I started getting thousands. I introduced a hashtag and every week #TuesdayTeamNews and #MusicalXI, #HospitalXI, #SummerXI or #MilitaryXI would trend on Twitter. The really popular ones go global. The last time we did a #FilmXI it was the number one trend (most talked-about thing) both globally and in the UK for almost three hours. People love a pun.

I began receiving emails asking for a list of all the teams we'd done. Random websites started collating all the entries and I had over a dozen offers from people volunteering their services as Tuesday Team News secretaries to collate the thousands of entries. I was sent pictures from offices where worked stopped for 20 minutes each Tuesday as employees got together to produce their finest puns in the boardroom.

As you look through the teams a few things will become apparent – Borussia Monchengladbach and Peter Odemwingie are remarkably fruitful pun material, and the simplest ones are often the best. Shearer is right, it does sound like a complete 'pile of rubbish' but it's quite a popular one.

Throughout this book I have included some of the best Team XIs from the last few years. Originally I was going to try to find the punsters who came up with each name but it proved almost impossible, so if you see one of yours in here, celebrate wildly, fist-pump like there's no tomorrow and feel free to tell all your friends about it. I can't thank you all individually but I'm grateful for your gazillions of suggestions over the years – please keep them coming. I have lost count of the number of times I have choked on a scone when reading through them.

If you are interested, here was the final Lord Of The Rings XI that started it all off, managed by Gandalf Ramsey.

Lord Of The Rings XI

Peter Smeagol
Gollum Davidson
Bobby Mordor (c)
Legolassana Diarra
Arwen Robben
Vinny Samwise
Theoden Walcott
Boromir Zenden
Jean-Pierre Pipin
Jan Aragorn of Hesselink
Saruman Kalou
Dwight Orc
Alfrodo Di Stefano

JOBS XI

Has all the talk of employment made you wonder what a Jobs XI would look like? No? Here it is anyway:

Team Name: Interview Milan
Reserves: Chartered Sevilla
Stadium: The New Dentist
Training Ground: Brick Layer Road

Management Team
Pep Security Guardiola
SecreTerry Venables

First Team
Jussi JaaskeLinesman
Gary Barrister
Bixente LizaraZookeeper (c)
Papa Bouba LolliDiop Lady
James Milliner
CV Gerrard
Ji-sung Car Park Attendant
Asamoah Gyanaecologist
Farmhando Torres
Pele Dancer
Aliadiere Hostess

Subs
Brickie Lambert	Cabbie Agbonlahor
Consiergio Aguerro	Kaka Dealer
Nanny	Gabriel Prostituta
Dentist Bergkamp	Cesc Fabregasman

DAVID WACKER

Most of the time I'm awake I am thinking about playing sport and all of my dreams are filled with scoring goals, sinking putts, hitting sixes and winning gold medals. I should point out that I can never remember dreaming of swimming-related glory. Although at 6ft 6in I have an obvious height advantage, while everyone else at school was learning the breaststroke and front crawl, I was pulling myself along using the tiles on the bottom of the pool and dunking my friends. During one 25-metre race in primary school my technical deficiencies in the pool came to a head. There was so much water being displaced that my teacher, Mrs Towers, thought I was having some sort of fit and alerted the lifeguard. He was midway through cranking up the OAP retrieval-crane when I surfaced and he realised it wasn't as serious as it looked.

I reached my sporting peak in my final year at Three Bridges Middle School by winning the tennis and table tennis tournaments, taking the 200-metre title, throwing a tennis ball further than anyone else, taking ten catches in one game of cricket and being part of the winning team in the rounders, softball, basketball and netball (don't ask) tournaments. I even managed to win the school chess tournament (although there were only half a dozen competitors – four of whom were forced to take part as a punishment, and one other who crumbled under the pressure of the final, sweating profusely and then crying when I took his queen after only four moves). That year everything I touched turned to gold.

The defining moment in my football career took place a few years later at secondary school. The team at Hazelwick had some serious quality. More than half of them played for the county and four or five would go on to have trials to play professionally. After a couple of seasons running around in such exalted company I was beginning to realise that perhaps I wasn't good enough to play football for a living.

One incident in particular sealed my footballing future. Our school team reached the final of the Sussex County Cup against archrivals Thomas Bennett. The game was attended by hundreds of kids from each school and I scored two goals in a 4-2 victory – my greatest night on a football pitch. One of them was a tap-in from three inches and the other came off my face, but it matters not. The report of the game made the inside pages of the *Crawley Observer* that weekend. I rummaged through the paper at 200mph trying to find my name and to my horror... this is what I saw: 'The game came to life in the second half with two goals coming from Hazelwick's David Wacker.'

slightly confused about which sport I like

My heart sank. The biggest moment of my football career and no one knew it was me! I want you to imagine a crushed 14-year-old who has just seen his chosen path in life crumble around him. That was me... for at least a week. When I look back to that deeply sad day I like to think there is still a scout from Barcelona out there somewhere searching for David Wacker. If anyone ever asks you if you know of Mr Wacker, Spanish accent or otherwise, please point them in my direction.

THE TALLEST AND SHORTEST FOOTBALLERS EVER

I was lucky enough to enjoy a slight height advantage in my youth. In my early schooldays I used to score loads of headers while opponents were tugging at my shin pads but I was by no means the tallest footballer ever to play the game. Here's a look at the beautiful game's most beautiful specimens, both high and low.

TALLEST

7'0"
Kristof van Hout (Genk GK) 2.08m (6ft 10in)
Yang Changpeng (Chengdu Blades) 2.06m (6ft 9in)
6'6"
Tor Hogne Aaroy (ex-Aalesund, Norway) 2.04m (6ft 8in)
Peter Crouch 2.02m (6ft 7in)
6'0"
Jan Koller 2.02m (6ft 7in)
Nikola Zigic 2.02m (6ft 7in)
5'6"
Kostas Chalkias (ex-Portsmouth GK) 1.99m (6ft 6in)
Zat Knight 1.98m (6ft 6in)
5'0"

SHORTEST

4'6"
Jafal Rashed (Al Sadd, Qatar) 1.55m (5ft 1in)
4'0"
Daniel Villalba (Argentina youth international) 1.57m (5ft 2in)
Elton Jose Xavier (Al Nasr, Saudi Arabia) 1.58m (5ft 2in)
3'6"
Levi Porter (ex-Leicester) 1.60m (5ft 3in)
Alan Wright 1.63m (5ft 4in)
3'0"
Aaron Lennon 1.65m (5ft 5in)

Crouch and Lennon: too awkward for high-fiving

NEWCASTLE MANAGERS' NAME MISPRONUNCIATION MASTERCLASS

On reflection, David Wacker is really quite acceptable – especially when you revisit some of these howlers from Joe Kinnear and Bobby Robson, both of whom happen to be former Newcastle managers. Let's kick off with the Godfather of Gobbledegook, Joe Kinnear.

JOE KINNEAR

Jonas Gutierrez = Jonas Gaultierrez

Charles N'Zogbia = Charles Insomnia

Yohan Cabaye = Yohan Kebab

Shola Ameobi = Shola Amamobi

Hatem Ben Arfa = Hatem Ben Afri

Papiss Cisse = Sissy

Derek Llambias (former Newcastle managing director) = Derek Lambezi

BOBBY ROBSON

Wayne Rooney = Mickey Rooney

Shola Ameobi = Carl Cort

Bryan Robson = Bobby Robson

Sir Bobby to Bryan: 'Good morning Bobby.'
Bryan: 'You're Bobby, I'm Bryan!'

Funny Football Transfers

After my – well, David Wacker's – brace in the Sussex County Cup final, my transfer value shot through the roof. There were definitely managers considering offering me a sandwich and a packet of crisps for my services; unfortunately, none of the could find the real me. All this led me to look into some of the most unusual football transfers in history – and I don't mean Liverpool buying Andy Carroll for £35 million. No, these were far stranger...

DANIEL ALLENDE: CENTRAL ESPANOL TO RENTISTAS

Allende's agent called to tell him he'd arranged a meaty contract for him at Rentistas – he joined the Uruguayan club for 550 steaks, to be paid in instalments of 25 steaks a week.

TONY CASCARINO: CROCKENHILL TO MILLWALL

One of Ireland's finest got his dream move to the Lions for a set of tracksuits.

GARY PALLISTER: BILLINGHAM TO MIDDLESBROUGH

England's future defensive colossus moved to Boro for a set of kit, a bag of balls and a goal net. No image rights negotiation here.

KENNETH KRISTENSEN: VINDBJART TO FLOEY

The Norwegian Third Division club received their star striker's weight in shrimps for this move.

ZAT KNIGHT: RUSHALL OLYMPIC TO FULHAM

Rushall's players were kept warmer on match days after Fulham gave the club 30 tracksuits in exchange for Knight.

ERNIE BLENKINSOP: CUDWORTH TO HULL

Hull paid Cudworth £100 and a barrel of beer for Blenkinsop in 1921. Reports that Cudworth lost their next match 16-0 because their players were drunk remain unconfirmed.

IAN WRIGHT: GREENWICH BOROUGH TO CRYSTAL PALACE

The Arsenal and England great got his break into the Football League by virtue of Palace giving Borough a set of weights for his services.

PLAYER UNKNOWN: GILLINGHAM TO ASTON VILLA

Records have misplaced the name of the player, but we do know that the Gills received three turnstiles, two goalkeepers' jerseys, three cans of weedkiller and a typewriter in exchange for the mystery man. Perhaps the greatest anonymous transfer in history.

JOHN BARNES: SUDBURY COURT TO WATFORD

The England legend arrived at Vicarage Road at about the same time as a full set of football kit turned up at Sudbury Court.

MARIUS CIOARA: UT ARAD TO REGAL HORNIA

The Romanian defender's transfer fee was 15kg of pork sausages, but Cioara decided to retire a day later, leaving Hornia demanding their sausages back. I am massively disappointed that I haven't been able to find out if the sausages were ever returned. Someone call *Panorama*.

THE FOOTBALLERS WHO WERE ALMOST NOT FOOTBALLERS

Most footballers are annoying because they are doing something we'd all like to be paid for but some are also aggravatingly good at any sport they turn their hand to. Some almost ended up doing something very different...

WAYNE ROONEY

The Manchester United hitman could have used that very nickname in the boxing ring if he'd followed his childhood dream. Rooney's former Liverpool schoolboys team-mate, Chris Dagnall, says: 'He used to say he didn't want to be a footballer when he grew up, he wanted to be a boxer.'

JOE HART

The England goalkeeper was a very good cricketer in his teens, so much so that he spent two years in the Worcestershire cricket academy developing his bowling skills. Hart's coach, Damian D'Oliveira, says: 'I am sure he would have been good enough to play county cricket. In fact, I think he would have been a very good county player.'

THEO WALCOTT

He only came to football at the age of ten, but Theo could easily have chosen athletics instead of the beautiful game. With a 100m time of 10.3 seconds, Walcott might have been an Olympian. 'I think if I'd had the training, I probably could have been a sprinter,' he admits.

At the shoe shop with Theo

ANDY GORAM

Another goalkeeper with a talent for the smaller ball game, Goram turned out for Scotland's national cricket team four times between 1989 and 1991, but was forced to abandon his alternative career due to injury concerns.

ZLATAN IBRAHIMOVIC

The Swedish striking sensation might have used his talents in the world of martial arts as he was a very promising taekwondo star in his youth, winning a black belt at the age of 17. But, as is always the case in this section, he chose football. Imagine what life would be like without the perpetual discussion about whether he's actually any good?

GEOFF HURST

Imagine a world in which Hurst had been a cricketer? Say goodbye to 1966 and all that... maybe there would never have been people on the pitch at all! Fortunately, Hurst gave up cricket in 1964 after playing a County Championship match, and more than 20 second-string games, for Essex. Phew.

GARY LINEKER

Another cricketer – well, it is our summer sport after all – who ended up in football. Gary captained the Leicestershire Schools team from the age of 11 to 16 and once said: 'I thought at the time I would probably have more chance afterwards in cricket than football.' Fortunately, he was wrong.

CURTIS WOODHOUSE

The former England Under-21 midfielder was a keen boxer in his youth. 'Boxing has always been my first love,' he says. 'When I was a kid, most lads' heroes were Paul Gascoigne and John Barnes but mine were Mike Tyson and Nigel Benn. I went from scrapping in the street and at school to fighting in the boxing ring from the age of twelve.' Amazingly, Woodhouse retired from football at the age of 26 to pursue his boyhood dream of being a boxer, and ended up winning the British light-welterweight title in 2014.

Golf XI

So what offering from the world of Tuesday Team News do we put at the end of this chapter? I thought long and hard about it and opted for a Golf XI for the following three reasons:

1) Most footballers would love to be golfers.
2) I like golf.
3) When the publishers first asked me to think about this book I said if it went into publication without Backspin Shinawatra included it would be a disgrace.

So here we go...

Team Name: Borussia Monchengladback 9
Reserves: 5&4Far Athletic
Stadium: 3 Wood Park

Management Team
Joe Royle & Ancient
Graham Taylor Made
Get In The Jol

Chairman
Backspin Shinawatra (there he is)

First Team

Rio Birdieland	Hole-In-Wanchope
Gimme Traore	Ibrahim Back9ayoko
Fade Elliott	Peter Odemswingie
Dogleg Luzhny (c)	Pitch-And-Puttrescu
Caddyshaka Hislop	Benni McParthree
Joan HandiCapdevilla	

Subs

Edwin Under Par	Nwankwo Kanoustie
Park Ji-Sunningdale	RideOut Of Bounds
Marc OverPars	Gabby Flagbonlahor

Golf: the more I practise, the more inept I become

FOOTBALL AND POLITICS

We'll look at the royal involvement in football later but only a short, heavily armoured car ride away from Buckingham Palace is the home of the prime minister. I remember interviewing Gordon Brown on a tram in Manchester in the build-up to the 2008 European Championships.

He talked about how England winning a major tournament during your time in office would guarantee you another election win – even if you're Scottish!

Mr Brown is a proud and genuine fan of Raith Rovers. You can't fake knowledge of Andreas Herzog's own goal in the Olympic Stadium in Munich in 1995. I remember talking to him about the 6-5 penalty win over Celtic in the final of the League Cup the season before – a victory that set up the game against Bayern Munich. Let's not forget, the mighty Rovers were 1-0 up at half time.

The problem for politicians is that all football fans are incredibly sceptical when it comes to those in power putting their

With a former number ten at Number 10

hooks into the beautiful game. Unless you can back it up with knowledge like the big G.B., the freshly ironed photo-shoot football scarf and 'I really like soccer' quotes are a dead giveaway.

Legend has it that David Cameron is a fan of Aston Villa. When, a few years ago, I went to speak to him at Number 10 about England's failed World Cup bid I did consider asking him to pick Gordon Cowans out of a line-up, but as we were setting up in Winston Churchill's old office we were paid a visit by Mr Cameron's communications director, Andy Coulson.

He was doing his job making sure I wasn't going to bowl him any googlies and that we were sticking to the script as far as the questions were concerned.

'Don't ask him too much about Villa, will you?' was the suggestion from Brother Coulson. In the end Mr Cameron acquitted himself very well and was some way short of the embarrassment factor that Tony Blair produced when he came on *Football Focus* and claimed that Arjan de Zeeuw was his favourite footballer.

If ever a prime ministerial aide was having a joke, that was surely it.

Despite DeZeeuwgate our former prime minister is a watcher of football. I discovered this after we did a show on the road at Burnley's Turf Moor during their last time in the Premier League, under Owen Coyle. Confirmed Claret Alastair Campbell was one of our guests alongside England cricketer Jimmy Anderson.

After the show we were invited to watch the match in the directors' box and sat down for some posh nosh. Anderson showed his true Lancashire class, passing on the rhubarb crumble and asking for pure custard. He ate it clean and mentioned that it was the secret to long tours abroad.

During the custard course, Mr Campbell turned his phone back on and in came the texts from various people, including one from 'Tony'. Campbell opened the text, laughed and turned the phone to Jimmy and me.

'I hope you were watching *Football Focus*. It was all about Burnley!' 'Tony' had clearly missed Alastair's section in the show but it was good to know that the most powerful people in the world like to keep up to date with the world's most popular sport. The call has already gone in for Barack Obama to sit alongside Alan Shearer on *Match of the Day*.

POLITICAL FOOTBALLERS WHO MADE A STATEMENT ON THE PITCH

For all those who try to keep politics (and politicians) out of football, some footballers have been determined to use the pitch as a way of raising awareness. Which is nice but against the rules.

ROBBIE FOWLER

As well as the famous 'snorting' incident, Mr Fowler employed another more meaningful goal celebration – which also landed him in hot water. During a 1997 European Cup Winners' Cup tie against Brann Bergen, the former Liverpool striker revealed a t-shirt underneath his kit that displayed the following message: 'Support The 500 Sacked Dockers' – a reference to the ongoing Liverpool dock workers' dispute. UEFA then revealed a message of its own to Fowler: pay us 2,000 Swiss francs for making an on-pitch political gesture.

PAOLO DI CANIO

The fiery Italian is no stranger to controversy and he might have got just a little carried away after a Lazio match in Rome. Walking off the pitch in just his trademark vest after a 3-1 derby win over Roma, Di Canio gave a straight-armed fascist salute to Lazio fans, for which he was banned by the Italian FA. Di Canio has gone on record as saying he was 'a fascist, not a racist' and wrote in his autobiography: 'I think he [Mussolini] was a deeply misunderstood individual. He deceived people. His actions were often vile. But all this was motivated by a higher purpose. He was basically a very principled individual.' Thank you, Paolo.

ENGLAND

When the England team went to Berlin in 1938 to play a friendly against Germany, they became embroiled in an infamous political incident. The British ambassador requested that the players perform the Nazi salute before kick-off 'as a courtesy', causing uproar in the England dressing room, which included Stanley Matthews and Cliff Bastin. The players were told that not saluting would cause a diplomatic incident and so they eventually relented, handing Hitler a major propaganda coup, followed by a 6-3 drubbing.

GIORGOS KATIDIS

Staying with Nazi salutes, AEK Athens midfielder Giorgos Katidis scored the winning goal against Veria in 2013 and celebrated with a... well, you can imagine. The Greek authorities took no chances and banned the former Greece Under-21 captain from international football for life as well as fining him 50,000 euros. AEK also banned him for the rest of the season, at which point he left the club for good.

PAUL GASCOIGNE

During his time at Rangers, Gazza celebrated scoring an Old Firm goal by pretending to play a flute right in front of the Celtic fans. This seemingly innocuous gesture was actually a Loyalist symbol and, although Gazza protested his innocence and claimed somebody had told him to do it, he was fined £20,000 and subjected to IRA death threats.

AHMED ABD EL-ZAHER

El-Zaher was playing for Egyptian club Al Ahly in the African Champions League final when he made a four-fingered salute to fans – widely recognised as an Islamist gesture in support of the Egyptian opposition. He was subsequently suspended without pay.

Political Footballs – When MPs and Football Collide

I'm all for genuine Alastair Campbell-style passionate football fervour from political types, but sometimes the two worlds of football and politics just don't work well together.

Tony Blair

He may have meant well when he texted Alastair Campbell about *Football Focus*, but Blair's most infamous footballing foray was his cringeworthy keepy-uppies with Newcastle manager Kevin Keegan in 1995. To his credit, the soon-to-be prime minister wasn't too bad (with his knees), but he fooled nobody when he held a Newcastle scarf aloft as if he'd been a Gallowgate regular since he was a nipper. Haddaway, man.

David Miliband

Staying in the North-east, the political world held its breath waiting to see what Miliband's next move would be after losing out to his brother in the 2010 Labour leadership election. Amazingly, he took up a board position at Sunderland – although he stopped short of holding up a scarf in the centre circle. He stayed for two years until the club appointed Paolo Di Canio as manager, and the former foreign secretary resigned in protest at the Italian's extreme political views (see page 31).

Helen Grant

The Tory sports minister must have thought she was on to a winner when she attended a hockey match to help publicise tax breaks for sports clubs in 2013. But she was left with egg on her face when a local ITV news crew gave her an impromptu quiz in which she failed spectacularly, getting every question wrong, including the identity of the current FA Cup holders. 'Come on, help!' she answered. 'FA Cup holders? FA Cup holders? Manchester

United because it is my favourite club.' Sadly for Helen, and all football fans, it doesn't work like that. It was Wigan.

Gordon Brown

It pains me to include the former PM on this list because the man is a devoted Raith Rovers fan, and even used to sell programmes outside the ground when he was a child. But he caused serious damage to the cringeometer in the build-up to the 2010 general election when he attacked the Conservative Party with a football chant: 'There is a football slogan which people shout from the terraces at the management. "You don't know what you're doing." That is what the Conservative position really is. They just don't know what they are doing.' Stop it, Gordon.

Boris Johnson

Never mind Keane on Haaland or Thatcher (Ben, not Margaret) on Mendes, when it comes to live TV's most shocking tackle of all time there is only one winner – the Mayor of London. In 2006, Boris was playing in a televised charity match alongside English legends against their German counterparts. Only somebody forgot to tell BoJo that he was playing football, not rugby, as he steamed into Maurizio Gaudino, with a rare 'cranium to the nads' spear tackle which left his opponent in a crumpled heap. The YouTube footage of the incident actually gets funnier with each viewing – and, yes, I am responsible for the bulk of its three million hits.

David Cameron

While I'm sure Dave's passion for Villa is entirely genuine, he didn't exactly endear himself to his fellow Holte-Enders when he pontificated on his side's chances of avoiding relegation in 2011. 'The Governor of the Bank of England, who's a Villa supporter, told me that Villa tend to do better when the economy is doing badly. I hope Villa doing badly is a sign of better economic times to come.' Fortunately for the PM, he was wrong as Villa stayed up – and so did the economy.

Jack Straw

The former Labour cabinet minister had a brainwave to get the home nations' football teams back at the top of the international game: 'The one area of sport where we have been consistently successful is athletics and that is the one area of sport where we do not have an English, Scottish and Welsh team but a British team. I personally look forward to the day when we have a British football team. I think we might start winning some games.' Unsurprisingly, that idea was dismissed and laughed off by football fans across Great Britain, meaning Straw did succeed in uniting the nation after all.

Barack Obama

The leader of the free world let himself down when he broke football's golden rule: never change your team. On a trip to London in his pre-presidential days, perhaps persuaded by his half-sister's West Ham-supporting English husband, Obama took in a game of football at Upton Park and became a Hammers fan for life. Or until he was sent a shirt from a fan of Al Wasl, when he promptly ditched the Iron and sent a message of support to the Dubai side, wishing them success in all competitions.

FOOTBALL'S GREATEST POLITICIAN – SEPP BLATTER'S
BEST QUOTES

None of the great political names featured in this chapter so far comes even close to holding a candle to the beautiful game's ultimate politico. Blatter has never been afraid to say what he thinks and here is a collection of some of the world's 'favourite' Blatterisms. And remember, people... he's in charge!

ON RACISM (2011)
'We are in a game, and at the end of the game, we shake hands, and this can happen, because we have worked so hard against racism and discrimination.'

ON WOMEN'S FOOTBALL (2004)
'Let the women play in more feminine clothes like they do in volleyball. They could, for example, have tighter shorts. Female players are pretty, if you excuse me for saying so, and they already have some different rules to men – such as playing with a lighter ball. That decision was taken to create a more female aesthetic, so why not do it in fashion?'

ON MULTI-MILLIONAIRE FOOTBALLERS (2008)
'I think in football there's too much modern slavery in transferring players or buying players here and there, and putting them somewhere.'

ON GAY FANS PLANNING TO ATTEND THE 2022 QATAR WORLD CUP (2010)
'I would say they should refrain from any sexual activities.'

ON ITALIAN MATCH-FIXING (2006)

'I could understand it if it had happened in Africa, but not in Italy.'

ON BANNING DRAWS (2004)

'Every game should have a winner. When you play cards or any other game, there's always a winner and a loser. We should have the courage to introduce a final decision in every game of football.'

ON MOVING THE GOALPOSTS (1996)

'The guardians of the rules are in agreement to lengthen the goals by the diameter of two balls, around 50cm, and to increase the height by the diameter of one ball.'

ON JOHN TERRY'S ALLEGED AFFAIR WITH A TEAM-MATE'S PARTNER (2010)

'If this had happened in, let's say, Latin countries then I think he would have been applauded.'

ON FIFA'S FEMALE BOARD MEMBERS (2013)

'We now have three ladies on the board. Say something, ladies. You are always speaking at home, say something now.'

Sepp Blatter unveils controversial tiny football

Unlikely European Adventures

When talking about the incredible European dream seasons experienced by British clubs, there's no better starting point than Gordon Brown's Raith Rovers. This one's for you, former PM.

Raith Rovers v Bayern Munich, 1995

The Kirkcaldy minnows won the League Cup the season before to seal their place in the UEFA Cup, and then came through the preliminary and first rounds before taking on the mighty Germans. Sadly, they lost the first leg 2-0 at Hibernian's Easter Road, but they then astonishingly took the lead in Munich thanks to Danny Lennon's deflected free kick. They eventually lost the second leg 2-1, but when you consider the German team contained the likes of Kahn, Helmer, Ziege, Hamann, Zickler, Scholl and Klinsmann, leading in Bavaria wasn't a bad effort.

Millwall v Ferencvaros, 2005

Reaching the 2004 FA Cup final was enough to secure a UEFA Cup spot for the Lions, then in the second tier, despite subsequently losing in the Cardiff final. Their reward was a tie with the Hungarian side and they drew their first ever European game at home, but went down 3-1 in the second leg.

Norwich v Bayern Munich, 1993

Nobody gave Mike Walker's Norwich side a prayer when they were drawn against Munich in the UEFA Cup, especially the Germans

TNS v Manchester City… and the world's first keeper with a football for a face

who completely underestimated the Norfolk side. But City duly won 2-1 in the Olympic Stadium – the first English club ever to win there – and secured a 1-1 home draw to defeat the European giants. But the dream ended in the next round when the Canaries suffered two narrow defeats to Inter Milan.

Bala Town v Levadia Tallinn, 2013

Ten years earlier, Bala had been playing parks football in the Wrexham region of the Welsh National League but a rapid rise meant the club from a village with a population of under 2,000 qualified for Europe via the Welsh Premier League. With only 504 seats in their ground, Bala were forced to play their first ever European tie at Rhyl, which, amazingly, they won 1-0 against the then Estonian league leaders, only to slip up 3-1 in the second leg.

Total Network Solutions v Manchester City, 2003

The New Saints of Oswestry Town and Llansantffraid FC were known by their sponsored name between 1997 and 2006, and drew City in a UEFA Cup qualifying round tie in 2003, going down 7-0 on aggregate. Two years later, they fared marginally better against Liverpool in a Champions League qualifying first-round tie, losing 6-0 on aggregate against the defending European champions.

Linfield v CSKA Sofia, 1967

The Northern Irish champions shocked the continent by reaching the last eight of the European Cup, after beating Aris and

Valerenga in the first two rounds. Unfortunately, the might of CSKA Sofia proved too much for them as they lost 3-2 on aggregate.

Aberdeen v Real Madrid, 1983

The night that Sir Alex Ferguson claimed his first European trophy will never be forgotten by any Aberdeen fan, especially given the lack of success for the proud club since that glorious Fergie-inspired era. A famous Cup Winners' Cup quarter-final win over Bayern Munich helped them on their way to the final against Alfredo di Stefano's Real. Fergie gave the Argentine star a bottle of single malt whisky before the match, and the rest is history as John Hewitt's extra-time header gave the Dons a 2-1 win.

Cefn Druids v MyPa, 2012

It might sound like a *Game of Thrones* battle, but this was actually a Europa League qualifying tie between the Welsh underdogs and the Finnish top-flight side. Druids were the first ever Welsh second-tier club to make it into Europe as cup runners-up, and they even held their opponents to a goalless draw in the first leg at Wrexham's Racecourse Ground, before a 5-0 thrashing in Finland.

Wrexham v Porto, 1984

Arguably the most astonishing achievement by any British club in Europe saw Fourth Division (that's League 2 to some of you) Wrexham stun the Portuguese giants in the Cup Winners' Cup first round. The Welsh Cup runners-up already set tongues wagging with a 1-0 first leg win against the competition's beaten finalists from the previous season. But the best was to come in Portugal, as Wrexham came from 3-0 down to fight back to 3-2 and an aggregate lead. They fell a further goal back, only for a then unknown Barry Horne to grab another goal for a 4-3 defeat and an utterly incredible away-goals win. Unfortunately, a second-round tie against Roma proved too much for the Welsh club, but after Porto, it didn't really matter.

Finger-licking Football Food

Jimmy Anderson enjoyed his Turf Moor custard, but he's missing out on some veritable signature dish treats across the UK's football grounds.

SCOTCH PIE

A Carlisle United staple, consisting of minced lamb and vegetables in a thick shortcrust pastry case. Don't be fooled by the name – Carlisle is in England.

AGGBOROUGH SOUP

Worth the trip to watch Kidderminster Harriers alone, this hearty broth will warm you up whatever the weather or team performance.

THE THIERRY HENRY PIE

Only available at Piebury Corner, near Arsenal's Emirates Stadium, the pie deli serves many items named after former Gunners, including Henry's, which is filled with venison in red wine gravy. How very London.

PORK ROLL

Lincolnshire is synonymous with its pork dishes, and if you take a trip to Sincil Bank on a match day, a hot pork roll with either stuffing or apple sauce can be yours alongside a ticket to watch Lincoln City.

POTTS PIES

Head to Morecambe for what are reputedly the best steak and ale pies – served up on a plate with mushy peas – in English football... according to 93 judges at the British Pie Awards, anyway.

INFAMOUS

FOOTBALL FOOD

Like you lot, I go pretty large on how much I like food, but just occasionally the stuff that keeps us going every day has played a wicked role in football events.

PIZZAGATE

When Manchester United ended Arsenal's 49-match unbeaten Premier League run in 2004, the Gunners players refused to go down without a fight – in the tunnel. What followed was the 'Battle of the Buffet', as the post-match fuel was used as ammunition with Fergie himself having a large slice of pizza hurled in his direction, staining his jacket in the process. The culprit has never been officially revealed, but Cesc Fabregas has never denied it. Nudge, nudge, wink, wink.

PIEGATE I

Incredibly, that wasn't the only time that Sir Alex was the innocent victim of a food fight. In 2009, the United Under-18 squad performed its traditional festive panto at the club's Christmas lunch, which then descended into an anarchic mince pie fight with the gaffer taking one squarely in the face.

LASAGNEGATE

Now officially banned from sale at White Hart Lane forever (probably), the Italian dish once cost Spurs a Champions League place – and about £10 million in the coffers. Going into the final game of the 2005/06 season, Tottenham led their archrivals Arsenal in the battle for fourth place. If Spurs were to win at West Ham, they would end an 11-year wait to finish above the Gunners as well as qualify for the Champions League. But the night before the game, the Spurs squad tucked into the buffet at their hotel in Canary Wharf and, within hours, at least ten of them were vomiting – and not with nerves. The common denominator was thought to be lasagne and, despite some frantic, last-ditch attempts to move the kick-off or have the game postponed, Martin Jol's food-poisoned side took to the pitch and lost 2-1, while Arsenal beat Wigan to nick fourth place. Ouch.

MEXICANGATE

It's still a mystery. Nobody knows what caused England goalkeeper Gordon Banks's mysterious stomach bug on the eve of the 1970 World Cup quarter-final in Mexico. But what we do know is that it may well have cost England a place in the World Cup final. At least. Banks was struck with the puzzling ailment the night before England's last-eight tie against West Germany. Having to spend prolonged spells in the toilet in football's first known case of squeaky-bum time (sorry) meant that Banks had to be replaced by Peter Bonetti, who proceeded to have a bit of a shocker. England were coasting at 2-0 up in the second half, when Franz Beckenbauer's shot somehow squirmed its way underneath poor Peter and the game changed. A weird looping backwards header from Gerd Muller somehow flew over Bonetti, before the same man scored from close range in extra time to seal England's fate. Would England have lost if Banks was playing? Who knows. But as manager Sir Alf Ramsey said: 'Of all the players to lose, we had to lose him.'

PIEGATE II

Mick Quinn was a phenomenal top-flight goalscorer, and he was also a tad round, meaning he was subjected to routine derogatory chants from opposition fans. Once, in a game for Newcastle, Quinn had a pie thrown at him so he promptly took a bite and carried on playing.

PIEGATE III

Neil Ruddock was fond of a steak and kidney pie back in his playing days. In fact, he probably still is. When he was playing for Liverpool, he kept a food diary to help him monitor his eating habits, and it was discovered that 'Razor' ate no fewer than 212 of the pies in one year.

OVEREATINGGATE

Like all players, Shinji Kagawa likes to tuck into the post-match buffet to refuel. Unlike all players, though, the Japanese international once overdid it ever so slightly. After Manchester United's 2013 defeat to Everton, Kagawa indulged in a bit of comfort eating, which ended with him in hospital having his stomach pumped after chomping way too much. He was even rested for United's next game amid concerns he hadn't fully recovered.

TANGERINEGATE

Blackpool fans, whose club play in tangerine – not the fruit, the colour of their kit – hurled hundreds of the fruit (and a load of tennis balls) on to the Bloomfield Road pitch in protest at owner Karl Oyston during a derby match against Burnley in 2014. Play was delayed, but on the plus side the players didn't have to leave the pitch for their half-time oranges.

POLITICAL XI

The Political XI was first thrown out there during the last general election and produced some absolute beauties. More recently, the rise of UKIP has been bad for staunch Europeans but wonderful for lovers of the pun.

Team Name: Faragentina
Reserves: UKIPswich Town
Stadium: Private Eyebrox
Training Ground: Nou Camp David

Management Team
Roberto DiploMatteo
Berti Votes

First Team
Friedel Of Speech
Joleon Prescott
Andy MP
Taribo Westminster
Eric Member-Member Of Parliament
Nanifesto
Ballack Obama (c)
BNPienaar
Peter LibDemWingie
Holyrood Van Nistelrooy
Liberal Cisse

Subs
Asmir Cleggovic
Lee Camp David
Erik BakkeBencher
Churchillian Petrov
Ronaldo Reagan

LETTERS FROM VIEWERS

We live in a technological age when people like to tell you what they think of you, your programme, your shirt, your hair, your nose etc in an instant via social media. It's always nice to get that insightful feedback and sometimes you know – like when Mark Lawrenson wears one of his magic-eye shirts on the TV – that you'll get a big response.

Over the years, though, I have found that if people really want to have a substantial moan they go old school and dig out the pen and ink. Obviously you do get some very nice complimentary letters. One lady went to great lengths to tell me that I reminded her of her late husband, and another asked how I managed to be in London on a Saturday for the football and Malaysia on the Sunday for Formula One. I wrote back to tell her that Jake Humphrey and I were not in fact the same person.

What I like about a letter is the level of detail that people go into. A few years ago I received one from a viewer who had simply had enough of my nose and decided to tell me about it.

Dear Mr Walker
After weeks of thinking about writing you a letter I finally decided to do it because last Saturday's 'Football Focus' was the final straw. I don't know if you are aware but your nose looks like a massive cashew nut or, at the very best, a deformed parsnip. Don't get me wrong, you're not a really ugly bloke or anything, and you can actually appear half-decent if you look straight down the camera but the problems start when you turn to the side.

When you look at your guests or the screen behind you I find myself unable to take my eyes off your conk. It makes you look like a male witch. It has got so bad that I have to call my wife in from the other room to ask her what she thinks. The good news is, she counts as one more viewer; the bad news is, she agrees with me.

I know this probably sounds cruel and heartless but I have been wanting to get this off my chest for a while. I am not going to suggest anything drastic like surgery but, for your own sake, make sure you only ever look straight down a camera.

Yours sincerely

Edward M

I wrote back to Edward to thank him – and his wife – for watching, as I did with a man called Paul who was a little peeved at my pronunciation of the word 'championship'.

Dear Mr Dan Walker

Normally I like to watch *Football Focus* on a Saturday with my family but your continued inability to pronounce a word correctly is making me gravitate towards a channel change.

Last week again you referred to Manchester United winning the 'championship'. Can I remind you that it is the CHAMPIONSHIP and not CHAMPIONCHIP.

The word has nothing to do with the fried potato, what some have on their shoulder or the technology that drives a computer.

I know this might seem like a small matter to you but it is beginning to send me a little mad. Can I encourage you to think about SHIPS rather than CHIPS?

Consider a boat, picture a yacht – anything that stops you from being quite so annoying.

I hope you take the time to read this and consider your actions. Otherwise – even if the rest of your programme is CHAMPIONSHIP quality – my family and I will be watching reruns of *Murder, She Wrote* on the other side.

Keep up the good work.

Paul

THE FOOTBALL FASHION DISASTER XI

Viewers are never afraid to give feedback on what we wear on the telly, especially those Lawro shirts, so here's a look at my 'favourite' football fashion nightmares. To each and every one of them, top marks for effort.

THE SPICE BOYS' SUITS

The original fashion disaster, as seen on the 1996 Liverpool FA Cup final squad. Steve McManaman, Robbie Fowler, David James et al paraded around the Wembley pitch in cream Emporio Armani suits before going on to lose to Manchester United. James was an Armani model at the time and the suits were rumoured to be his idea. Everyone else involved is keen to blame him at every opportunity.

DAVID BECKHAM'S SARONG

In 1998, when young David was photographed on a night out wearing a sarong, his fashion-icon status was set in stone forever. As was his presence in this section. He looked ridiculous but somehow got away with it. In 2012 he was asked about saronggate: 'I look back on some stuff and think, I can't believe I actually wore that.' Any child who wore a Campri ski jacket to school in the 1980s will feel his pain.

BARRY VENISON'S SHIRTS

There was a time in the 1990s when watching football meant you'd also have to put up with one of the former Liverpool star's absurdly colourful shirts – and his mullet. Thankfully, those days are no more as Barry emigrated to the USA to become a property developer. They love a mullet in the US of A.

DWIGHT YORKE'S SILVER SUIT

Of the many shirts Venison came up with, none were even close to the dazzling effect caused by Dwight Yorke's suit. The former Manchester United striker was a Sky Sports pundit for his old club's home game against Spurs in 2010, and shocked the football world with a shiny, all-silver number that made him look like he'd asked a tailor for the rare just-crossed-the-line-in-the-London-Marathon look.

TIM SHERWOOD'S GILET

It may lack the shock value of a silver or cream suit, but in its own way the former Spurs manager's sleeveless coat-thing – apparently known as a gilet – became a sight that caused sore eyes. Sherwood's passionate touchline style meant that he eventually dispensed with his gilet in dramatic fashion, slinging it down the tunnel during a home defeat to Arsenal.

DAVID SULLIVAN'S CLARET JACKET

'I know,' thought David Sullivan, on the morning of the press briefing announcing his Premier League club takeover in 2010. 'I'm going to wear a jacket that's the same colour as our shirts.' Which would have been fine if he had been taking over Chelsea or Everton, but proved to be a total shocker as his new club was West Ham. He occasionally attempts to distract attention from his claret-and-blue number by wearing his KGB hat.

CARSON YEUNG'S FUR COAT

The Birmingham owner decided to make the 2009 away trip to Liverpool a fancy-dress affair but committed the classic mistake of forgetting to tell anyone else, so stuck out ever so slightly in his Chewbacca outfit. Rumours had it that he was actually wearing a £30,000 Gucci original fur overcoat but that can't be true.

CRISTIANO RONALDO'S METALLIC DISCO PANTS

In the summer of 2008, Cristiano was recovering from injury so did what anyone in his condition would do – hang out in Los Angeles wearing a pink t-shirt, silver hotpants and white trainers, of course.

LIONEL MESSI'S POLKA DOT JACKET AND BOW TIE

Not to be outdone by his rival, Messi turned up to the 2013 Ballon D'Or awards sporting a polka-dotted jacket complete with matching bow tie. The blazer was designed exclusively for him by his sponsors, Dolce & Gabbana, and the look would set any ordinary punter back around £1,700.

JORGE CAMPOS'S GOALIE SHIRTS

David Seaman and Peter Schmeichel both sported their fair share of questionable keeper's jerseys in their time, but one man stood above all others when it came to custodian kits, and that was Mexico's Jorge Campos. He presumably employed a hyperactive, colour-blind two-year-old to come up with designs.

DJIBRIL CISSE'S, ER, CLOTHES

The French striker's off-pitch sartorial selections make the rest of this fantasy fashion team's efforts look fairly run-of-the-mill. Here is a man who wears blazers with nothing underneath, and even turned up to an awards do wearing a pair of Shakespearian baggy breaches and gloves, for no reason anybody could explain. When you are The Lord of Frodsham – a title that came with a property he bought in Cheshire – you can apparently do whatever you like when it comes to clobber.

FOOTBALLERS WHO PLAYED TWO GAMES IN 24 HOURS

Despite everyone thinking I could be in London for the football on Saturday and Malaysia for the Grand Prix on a Sunday, that is just not the case as, just to clarify, Jake Humphrey and I are different people. However, some footballers have pulled off even more amazing tricks, seemingly being in two places at once.

MARK HUGHES

If you have a look at the line-ups of Czechoslovakia v Wales, and Bayern Munich v Borussia Monchengladbach, both of which were played on 11 November 1987, you'll notice something strange. I appreciate you won't bother to have a look at those line-ups – why should you? – so let me do the hard work for you. Mark Hughes is listed as playing in both those games, not because there were two Mark Hugheses or because of a clerical error, but because he did actually appear in both games in different countries. After Wales lost 2-0 in a European Championship qualifier in Prague, Hughes was flown to Munich in a private jet where he came off the bench for Bayern in a German cup match. As if coming on with half an hour left wasn't tough enough for Hughes, the game also went into extra time, but at least his side came out on top.

SOREN LERBY

Bayern Munich are clearly a club who expect their players to give more than everything, as they had previous when it came to flying in players from international duty. In 1985, Denmark's Soren Lerby was helping his country to a 4-1 win against Ireland in Dublin, but was forced to leave the party after an hour in order to catch the Bayern private jet back to Germany. There, he came off the bench at half time for his side in a cup tie against Bochum which, amazingly, also went to extra time and finished all square.

JORGE CAMPOS

Our colourful-shirted goalkeeper is back, but this time it's for purely professional reasons as he played back-to-back matches on the same day, although no private jet was required. Campos appeared for LA Galaxy in a Major League Soccer game against Tampa Bay (Mutiny, if you must know) at the Rose Bowl in Pasadena in 1996 before changing into a different garish shirt and turning out for Mexico in an international against the USA at the same stadium.

CHRIS BALDERSTONE

But what Campos, Hughes and Lerby failed to do was play two different sports professionally on the same day. Anyone can jump into a private jet to play football, again. It takes a man of Balderstone's calibre to excel at football and cricket on the same day. In a feat most of us would only have achieved in our gardens as kids, in September 1975 Balderstone played county cricket for Leicestershire against Derbyshire, ending the day with an unbeaten 51, before dashing 30 miles up the road in a taxi to Doncaster Rovers' Belle Vue ground and playing in midfield in a 1-1 draw against Brentford. But that's not even the end of it. The following morning, Balderstone was back at Chesterfield and went on to make 116, and then took three wickets to help bowl Leicestershire to the victory that clinched the County Championship title.

CAN BARTU

Similar to Balderstone, but without the taxi dash, the promising Turkish midfielder scored two goals in a 4-0 win for Fenerbahce in January 1957, before heading off to the club's

basketball arena and contributing ten points towards his team's win that evening.

CANVEY ISLAND

It may lack the private jets, the multiple sporting achievements and a major piece of silverware, but Canvey Island's 2000/01 season finale is worthy of recognition nevertheless. Due to a combination of very bad winter weather, and extended cup runs, Canvey were forced to play their last eight league games in nine days, including their final five matches on successive days. The part-timers asked a huge amount of their players, including postman Mick Bodley, who still had to work throughout that period and said at the time: 'I had to laugh when I heard Gerard Houllier moaning about Liverpool's number of games. He should try playing eight games in nine days – and go out on the post every morning. I'm up at four-thirty, home at lunchtime, couple of hours' kip, out to football, back at midnight. And then I'll go and do it all again.' The happy ending to the story saw the team have a well-earned week off at the end of their league programme before winning the FA Trophy to have something to show for all their effort.

After eight games in nine days, Canvey Island celebrated a rare day off

FOOTBALL'S GREATEST NOSES

While Edward Marks may think my nose resembles a giant cashew nut or parsnip, he'd be utterly appalled to discover the conks of these footballing nasal heroes of mine.

Sasa Curcic (pre-nose surgery at Villa)

As Churchill once said of Russia, 'A riddle wrapped in a mystery inside an enigma.'

Steve Bruce

This is what happens when you spend your whole career being a hard-nosed (sorry) centre-back.

Steve Ogrizovic

The daddy of all football noses, the former Coventry goalkeeper had no fear when challenging in the box – as is clear.

Zlatan Ibrahimovic

An unorthodox rough diamond, much like its owner.

Matt Le Tissier
Southampton's finest.
Nose.

Gordon Cowans
The former Villa ace's nose
grew its own nose.

Phil Thompson
Another Anfield legend who
tries to avoid profile shots
wherever possible.

Giorgio Chiellini
Somehow the Italian's conk
covers almost his entire face.
Remarkable nasal scenes.

Ian Rush
The Anfield legend has
a legendary hooter.

Gareth Southgate
An unconventional
beauty but a beauty
nonetheless.

FAMOUS FOOTBALL CORRESPONDENCE

In light of my revealing the 'fan mail' sent to me, it's only fitting to conclude this part of the book with a look at some of football's most famous correspondence, from the poignant to the sublime, and a bit of the utterly ridiculous.

Vincent Tan to Malky Mackay

The controversial Cardiff City owner emailed a letter to his manager in December 2013, suggesting to him that he should resign his position or face the sack. Although the exact wording of the letter was never made public, it is 'understood' – in other words, someone who saw it told everyone – that Tan criticised Mackay's signings, transfer budget, results and style of play and his overall record as a manager. Other than that, he was fairly happy with him.

Sergeant Clement Barker to Montague Barker

On 29 December 1914, Sgt Barker wrote to his brother from the trenches of the First World War battlefields, and the contents of the missive proved the legendary no-man's-land football match between English and German soldiers definitely took place. Barker wrote:

> ... on the 24th had a messenger come over from the German lines and said that if they [our side] did not fire Xmas day, they (the Germans) wouldn't, so in the morning (Xmas day) a German looked over the trench – no shots – our men did the same, and then a few of our men went out and brought the dead in (69) and buried them and the next thing happened, a football kicked out of our trenches and Germans and English played football. Night came and still no shots. Boxing Day the same, and has remained so up to now...

Jose Mourinho to Chelsea Players

Soon after The Special One took over at Chelsea in 2004, he sent a letter to every member of his first-team squad, explaining what he needed from them to make a winning side. He'd done exactly the same thing when he'd first arrived at Porto in 2002. So, John Terry, Frank Lampard and Michael Essien were among the recipients of these words:

> From here each practice, each game, each minute of your social life must centre on the aim of being champions. First-teamer will not be a correct word. I need all of you. You need each other. We are a TEAM.
>
> Motivation + Ambition + Team + Spirit = SUCCESS.

Manchester United to Their Fans

In 2000, the Manchester United board took the decision to raise season ticket prices. They also took the decision to send a letter to all their season ticket holders explaining the price hike, and one of the reasons they gave was because club captain Roy Keane was being paid £52,000 per week. As you can imagine, Keane was ever so slightly irritated by this. This is what he said afterwards:

> I'm not one for holding grudges but this was a stupid mistake, a bad public relations exercise and something that should never have happened. I'm still waiting for my apology but I could be waiting a long time. The board have tried to explain what they meant, that it was part of a wider picture of trying to keep the fans informed, telling them the club wanted to rebuild and strengthen, which is why prices were going up. The fact is nobody should be singled out in a letter. It wasn't right. I felt everything was being laid at my door.

Roberto Mancini to Manchester City Fans

In one of the classiest moves of recent times, the departing Man City manager took out a full-page advertisement in the *Manchester Evening News* in 2013 to thank the City fans for their support. It read:

MANCHESTER CITY SUPPORTERS
3 UNFORGETTABLE YEARS
YOU WILL ALWAYS BE IN MY HEART
CIAO
ROBERTO MANCINI

And to show their appreciation, City fans returned the favour by taking out an ad in Italian newspaper *Gazzetta dello Sport*. More than 800 fans raised the £7,000 that was required to say:

Tony Pulis to Stoke Fans

Soon after Mancini's gesture, Pulis – who had been sacked by Stoke – wrote a letter to fans in local paper *The Sentinel*. It was pretty long, so here's part of it:

I am grateful for this opportunity here to express my gratitude because, unlike Roberto Mancini in his local paper last week, I can't afford to take out a full-page advert.

We have all been on one hell of a journey. It doesn't seem five minutes ago since I first went up to the Potteries for a 4-2 defeat at Walsall. In those days I think we had two sets of goals on the training ground and, if it ever rained, we were running round in puddles. On a match day, meantime, you could see more empty seats than occupied seats. But when I first arrived, I remember saying this was a proper football club with so much potential to do a lot better.

I will never forget the effort and the later celebrations as we won promotion back to the top division for the first time in 23 years.

A generation of Stoke fans had never seen their club play the best teams in the land week-in, week-out, so I can't tell you what it meant to be manager the day we did that.

Who can forget that first [Premier League] win against Aston Villa, not to mention the victories against a certain team from north London?

David Moyes to Manchester United Fans

In March 2014, as Manchester United's season continued to stutter under new manager David Moyes, he took the trouble to write to the club's season ticket holders and reassure them.

While I knew that this job would be a challenge when I took it on, the difficult season we have experienced was not something that I envisaged, which I am sure is the case as well for you supporters – and my players, staff and I are desperate to compensate for that.

You are accustomed to seeing a successful Manchester United and the backing you have given the players and me throughout the season has been incredible. Away from home the travelling fans have remained the best in the country while at Old Trafford your unwavering faith has been noticeable and hugely welcomed. Supporting your team when they are winning is easy but much harder when things are not going as well, and the loyalty you have shown us has been magnificent.

Despite the letter, Moyes was gone by April.

Steve Gibson to John Boileau

In recent years, it has become traditional for fans of the computer game *Football Manager* to make tongue-in-cheek applications for vacant managerial positions, citing their incredible virtual managerial achievements. And that's exactly what 25-year-old John Boileau did in May 2006 when Middlesbrough were looking for a new manager. He wrote about his magnificent, trophy-laden record in the game, and his stint in charge of a real Under-11 football team. Incredibly, Boileau received a reply from the Boro chairman Steve Gibson – and what a reply it was:

Dear John

Many thanks for your recent application for the managerial position at Middlesbrough Football Club.

You were of course the outstanding candidate but after careful consideration we decided against your appointment. Quite frankly, we were of the opinion that your tenure with us would have been short-lived as your undoubted talent would result in one of the big European clubs seeking your services.

We consider it a sign of our progress that someone of your status could consider us.

Yours
S GIBSON
CHAIRMAN

Alex Ferguson to Brian Howard

It's hard to believe now, but back in 1989 Fergie was fighting for his managerial future at Old Trafford. Luckily for him, he had an ally in fan Brian Howard, who wrote to his club's manager to offer him support. Ferguson's reply to the letter is below, but that's only half the story. A few months later, United won the FA Cup and Howard requested the manager's signature on the letter in a space underneath where he'd written '1990 FA Cup Winners'. For the next 23 years, every time United won a trophy, Howard returned to the United training ground, having made another space on Fergie's letter for the name of the trophy and the boss's signature. By 2013, he had a unique slice of history.

Here's that letter (minus the signatures):

Dear Brian
Many thanks for taking the time to come down to The Cliff and also for the kind letter.

I appreciated your letter very much as you like myself, regards United, care deeply for the club and just like you I get frustrated.

I have always been objective and know what I am trying to achieve but you have to overcome so many obstacles at our club that sometimes you wonder if there is a curse.

However, you must never give in and keep persevering and it will turn out right and then the press will have to think of something else to write about.

In the meantime, if we stand together then we will be stronger and that is what is needed.

Yours in Sport,
Alex Ferguson

Literature XI

I was once accosted by a serial Tuesday Team Newser outside a popular fast food establishment on Stevenage's old high street. He asked if I could do a Literature XI the following week because he had some excellent efforts he'd been holding on to for ages. I obliged and it produced a team of fine standing. Sadly, none of his suggestions made it but these are the ones that did...

Team Name: Enid Blyton & Hove Albion
Reserves: Alice In Sunderland
Stadium: Grisham Abbey

Management Team
Howard Kindle
Warnock & Peace
Poyet Laureate

First Team
20,000 Leagues Under The Seaman
Winnie The Puyol (c)
The Hungry Capdevilla
George OrwElokobi
Men Are From OverMars Woman Are From Jenas
The 3 McAteers
A.A. Milner
Much Edu About Nothing
Ibrahim HardBakayoko
One Flew Over Lukaku's Nest
The Lion The Witch And The AdebayorDrobe

Subs
BookCasey Keller
Ben Thatcher In The Rye
Of Mice & Mendieta
McBride & Prejudice
Ba From The Madding Crowd

Don Tiote
Captain Balotelli's Mandolin
Roald Dahl Tommason
1984Lan
Dr Dzeko & Graham Hyde

THE LONGEST WAITS

There are three questions I get asked with alarming regularity:
1. Have you ever met David Beckham?
2. Where does Lawro get his shirts from?
3. What is the worst thing about your job?

The answers are quite simple:
1. Yes, on numerous occasions.
2. I have no idea.
3. Waiting...

There are very few things to moan about in this line of work, but if you are someone who struggles to amuse yourself during hours of hanging around I would suggest that the world of broadcasting is not one you will particularly enjoy.

I once waited around for two solid days outside the Reebok Stadium for the result of Rio Ferdinand's missed drugs test hearing. During those two days I never once saw Rio Ferdinand but did consume something approaching 20 Filets-O-Fish.

When I first started out I would spend somewhere between one and four hours at Manchester United or Manchester City's training ground every single Friday morning. There is a squad picture outside the press room at Carrington and I am pretty sure I could tell you the position of every single player in it, having stared at it for that long. David May is sixth in from the right on the back row.

Paul Scholes always hated being interviewed and when it was his turn on the roster he would do everything he could to grind you down. I once turned up at 08:30 for a 09:15 slot with a couple of other local journalists. At 10:00 we were told he'd be there at 11:00. At 11:00 we were told he'd be there at 11:30. At 11:30 we were offered Mikael Silvestre instead... We declined.

Finally, at 11:45 we were reliably informed that Scholes had been tracked down and would be with us in two minutes. As we were being told that, the man himself drove past the entrance to the training ground and waved as he disappeared. Of course it was mildly annoying but then that was part of the magic of Paul Scholes – the man who seemingly hated all the baggage that came with football apart from the stuff that involved wearing boots.

An interview can still be painful even if your interviewee turns up just when they should. I remember a time at Wimbledon when I was due to speak to Venus Williams. After their matches the players go into the main press conference and then stroll across the corridor into a small room. As soon as they sit down you have two and a half minutes to conduct your TV interview. For one minute and 40 seconds Venus sat in silence, texting. 'Whenever you're ready, Miss Williams,' I interjected. She huffed, pressed send, and looked at me well aware that I had under a minute left. She produced two or three one-word answers and I asked her if there was anything she'd like me to ask her because she obviously wasn't interested in my questions. She said no. End of interview. It won't go down as one of my finest.

The world record holder for making you wait was Carlton Palmer, though. The long-legged former England midfielder had just been appointed as Stockport County's new manager back in 2001. I went down to the press conference on the day of his grand unveiling and was told that if I came back the following morning at eight the new manager would sit down with me before training.

I turned up at Edgeley Park the next day at 07:45 and was asked to wait in a little room to the side of the club shop. Unfortunately, I had forgotten to bring any knitting, *Angry Birds* hadn't been invented, the newsagent's was closed and there is only so long that *Snake* on a Nokia 3210 can keep you entertained. As the hours ticked by, I kept myself amused by seeing how many times I could throw a piece of rolled-up paper into a bin without missing. Just at the point when I was considering which arm I would eat if my hunger became uncontrollable, he turned up. It was nearly two-thirty in the afternoon.

In his first answer he told me that he fully expected to be England manager within five years. It was an answer worth waiting for but sadly for Carlton the FA never came calling and, after leaving Stockport, he had a brief spell in charge of Mansfield before exiting the dugout for good.

FOOTBALL'S LONGEST WAITS – A STATTO'S DREAM

My marathon wait for Carlton Palmer's pearls of wisdom seems like a matter of seconds when compared to some of the lengthy sentences handed down to the players, and fans, of these teams. Fact fans, start your engines...

38 GAMES WITHOUT A WIN

When Derby beat Newcastle 1-0 in the Premier League on Monday 17 September 2007, none of their fans would have realised the significance of that victory. It was to be the Rams' last league win for a staggering 38 matches, taking them all the way to the following season in the Championship, when they ended the sorry run with a 2-1 win against Sheffield United on Saturday 13 September 2008 – 362 days later.

28 YEARS WITHOUT A WIN

Success in football is relative. Derby fans would be unaware that they actually had it quite good when their win drought ended after a year, especially when compared to the South Pacific island nation of American Samoa. As documented in the superb film *Next Goal Wins*, their poor run started soon after their international football debut in 1983, and it took them until 2011 to win a match, when they beat Tonga 2-1.

American Samoa *not* winning another match – and on their way to a record 31-0 defeat to Australia

510 GAMES WITHOUT A GOAL

Even the most shot-shy defender pops up with the odd headed goal – but not Frank Womack, Birmingham City's full-back from 1908 to 1928. During that time, Womack turned out for the Blues 491 times, never once bothering to get on the score sheet. He moved to Torquay in 1929 where he made another 20 league appearances without scoring. For Frank, the wait never ended.

16 (S I X T E E N) POSTPONEMENTS

When the 1962/63 FA Cup third-round draw was made, Fourth Division Lincoln were at home to Third Division Coventry City. The tie was scheduled for Saturday 5 January, but the weather had other ideas. That winter saw a particularly large version of the big freeze and the tie was postponed no fewer than 16 times, before the game finally took place on Wednesday 6 March, two months later. It was worth the wait for Sky Blues fans, as they won 5-1.

TWO YEARS WITHOUT AN AWAY WIN

Leyton Orient's travelling fans had their patience tested beyond all reasonable standards as their team failed to win a single league game on the road between 30 October 1993, when they won 1-0 at Hull, and 12 September 1995, when they beat Northampton 2-1 at Sixfields. Amazingly, that was their only league success on the road for another year, until 10 September 1996 when they won at Northampton again.

171 GAMES WITHOUT A BORE DRAW

Fans of Peterborough United were treated to more than three years of entertainment as their team failed to serve up a single 0-0 stalemate between December 2009 and March 2013. When that glorious blank-out finally happened in a home match against Ipswich, the celebrations must have been wild.

12 GAMES WITHOUT A GOAL

Any team can go on a poor run, but few can manage it without even nicking the odd consolation goal. So hats off to Hartlepool who, in 1993, managed to go a wonderful 12 league and cup games without troubling the scorers.

36 YEARS WITHOUT PROMOTION OR RELEGATION

No fans would wish for relegation, but even Rochdale's most hardened supporters must have dreamed of leaving the Football League's bottom division one way or another just for a change of scenery. Between 1974 and 2010, the mighty Dale could not escape the basement, despite reaching the play-offs three times in the noughties. They finally won automatic promotion in 2010, before being relegated back into League 2 in 2012, and then going back up in 2014. They have now changed status to a yo-yo club.

91 GAMES WITHOUT BEING AWARDED A PENALTY

I'm not saying referees might have been biased against the up-and-at-'em tactics of Wimbledon, but the club went an astonishing 91 matches without being awarded a spot-kick, which would have made even the most reluctant conspiracy theorist a tad suspicious. The Dons' penalty against Leeds on 25 October 1997 was their last until 11 March 2000 when the ref pointed to the spot. And guess what happened? Neal Ardley scored.

131 GAMES WITHOUT BEING AWARDED A RED CARD

These days, you only have to have someone trip over your stray bootlace to pick up a red card, but there was a time when a little more was required for a player to be dismissed. So much so that Leeds United managed to go an incredible 131 games over three years in the early days of the Premier League without picking up a single red.

THE COMMENTS THAT CAME BACK TO HAUNT THEM

I'm all for bravado and good intentions from managers and players in the battle for success, but Carlton Palmer's claim that he would manage England within five years was pure nonsense – especially as he was sacked by his club less than two years later. And he wasn't the only one to set himself up for a fall.

RAFA BENITEZ

In 2007, the Liverpool manager went on record as saying the following about Chelsea: 'Chelsea is a big club with fantastic players, every manager wants to coach such a big team. But I would never take that job, in respect for my former team at Liverpool, no matter what. For me there is only one club in England, and that's Liverpool.' In 2012, Rafa accepted a job as Chelsea's interim manager. Some fans were a bit miffed.

Benitez on a beach with his dog. Man bends over in background

PAUL LAMBERT

Before his Aston Villa side were due to take on Sheffield United in the 2014 FA Cup, Lambert was asked if Premier League managers would prefer to avoid the competition. 'If they were being honest, they probably would do,' he said. 'Not just because of the money but survival in the league is vital.' Unsurprisingly, Villa were duly dumped out of the cup by their third-tier opponents, leaving Lambert to concentrate on the league.

ALAN PARDEW

Ahead of Newcastle's Europa League quarter-final tie against Portuguese side Benfica, Pardew infuriated the opposition with this appraisal of their team: 'Looking at the quality of the Benfica players and the fact that they are a Champions League team this year, plus they are already confirmed for Champions League next year, you have to say they would certainly be a top eight or ten team in the Premier League.' A 4-2 aggregate defeat soon followed and Benfica went on to reach the final.

GLENN HODDLE

'I am not sure whether he is a natural goalscorer,' said the England manager of the precocious young talent of Michael Owen. Hoddle did not start Owen at the 1998 World Cup for the first two games, but the youngster still managed to score from the bench against Romania. Then, in the second round against Argentina, Owen scored *that* goal and looked every bit a 'natural'.

KEVIN KEEGAN

Taking a break from managerial duties, Keegan was co-commentating on England's 1998 World Cup group game against Romania, and when Owen scored that late equaliser he said: 'When a game goes like this, there's only one team going to win it now, and that's England.' Romania obligingly scored an even later winner and King Kev was left looking a little daft.

ARSENE WENGER I

The Arsenal manager has always been bullish and in denial about transfer speculation, and in June 2011 he said: 'The Spanish press has been speculating about this for ages now. Let me be clear about this: Fabregas has been with Arsenal for a long time and he will stay here.' It won't surprise you to learn that later that summer, Cesc was off to Barcelona.

ARSENE WENGER II

That same summer, Wenger also pledged categorically to keep Samir Nasri: 'Samir's situation is clear for me. He stays. We are in a position where we can say no and we will, in the case of Samir... Imagine the worst situation, that we lose Fabregas and Nasri; you cannot convince people that you are ambitious after that.' Later that summer, Nasri joined Manchester City.

Sven makes a decent brew

GERMAN SCHADENFREUDE

Prior to England's 2001 World Cup qualifier in Germany, many of the hosts' great and good had their say on the visitors' chances. The Kaiser himself, Franz Beckenbauer, said: 'I am very sure that we are going to win this game. We are as good as, if not better than, Sven-Goran Eriksson's side. I am sure that we are better prepared for this match than England. We will beat England.'

Meanwhile, German striker Carsten Jancker pronounced: 'We don't have to worry about single players such as Michael Owen or Emile Heskey. We have a stronger team and that is what counts.' And midfielder Stefan Effenberg had this to say about relative England newcomer Steven Gerrard: 'Steven who? I don't know him. I am not interested in England, or who is in their squad. I don't have time. I have better things to do.' But they still weren't done yet, as German legend Uli Hoeness declared: 'How are England going to win in Germany? It hasn't happened for one hundred years. I have no doubts whatsoever that Germany will quite clearly thrash England. They will easily qualify for the World Cup with this match.'

As if I need to tell you, England won 5-1 with an Owen hat-trick and goals from Gerrard and Heskey. Sweet.

WAYNE ROONEY

Ahead of the first Manchester derby of 2013, Rooney told the *Daily Mirror* that matches between United and Liverpool were bigger than games against City: 'They're all big games. Obviously United and Liverpool has been a massive game over the years. City have had their success recently, but I would probably say that United and Liverpool is still the biggest game.' That didn't quite work out for Rooney as United were subsequently stuffed 4-1 at the Etihad.

NEIL WARNOCK

Before his Sheffield United side played at West Brom in 2001, Blades boss Warnock claimed that his players only had to stop Baggies strikers Lee Hughes and Jason Roberts to win the game. That incensed the rest of the Albion players, who went on to win 2-1, with goalscorer Ruel Fox saying: 'He really got us wound up when he emphasised all United had to do was to stop our front men and they were home and dry. That was all the motivation we needed. The rest of the team were even more determined to prove him wrong.'

ALAN HANSEN

Alan Hansen was famously forced to consume his own words after his *Match of the Day* declaration that 'you can't win anything with kids'. It was made in reference to the Manchester United side that lost their opening-day fixture of the 1995/96 season against Aston Villa, with Gary Neville, Phil Neville, Paul Scholes and Nicky Butt in the starting line-up. The summer before, the club had offloaded Mark Hughes, Paul Ince and Andrei Kanchelskis. Manchester United went on to do the double that year and Hansen's comment has been shouted back at him by thousands ever since. Despite that, he was actually right. As even the 'kids' themselves have acknowledged, success that season would never have arrived without the experience of players like Cantona and Bruce. So Hansen's large pie with 'humble' spelled out in pastry letters didn't taste as bad as many have made out.

PLEASE RETURN TO;
THE FOOTBALLERS WHO WENT AWOL

Paul Scholes would never shirk a challenge on the pitch, but as you've seen he loved to disappear without a trace when it was time to face the press. But there are some players whose vanishing acts were so good that nobody knew where they were for days. Even Mr Holmes would struggle with some of these bad boys...

THE MYSTERY OF THE MISSING CUBANS

When Cuba faced Canada in a World Cup qualifier in Toronto in 2012, you wouldn't have needed to be Pythagoras to work out that some of their players were missing. The Cubans fielded a starting XI, but not a single substitute as the bench was filled with coaches. Of the squad of 15 that arrived in Canada for the fixture, one was sick and three others had decided to make a new life for themselves over the border in America. For the record, Canada won 3-0.

THE MYSTERY OF THE VANISHING BLACK STARS

As Ghana's squad boarded a flight to Angola to play a 2009 friendly, three influential players were missing. Michael Essien, Sulley Muntari and Asamoah Gyan all failed to show up for the flight and were not contactable by phone, leaving Ghanaian officials fuming. When they finally tracked them down, each player was fined $5,000 and forced to issue an apology.

THE MYSTERY OF MIKEL'S DOUBLE DISAPPEARANCE

Lyn Oslo's highly coveted young midfielder John Obi Mikel had agreed a deal to sign for Manchester United – or so his Norwegian club thought. When he failed to turn up for training back in Norway, Lyn smelled a rat and it wasn't long before the Nigerian popped up in London, announcing that he was desperate to sign for Chelsea instead. To add to the confusion, Mikel then joined up with the Nigerian Under-20 World Cup squad, from which he also disappeared and was subsequently fined.

THE MYSTERY OF THE ABSENT MANAGER

Players may come and go as they please (and get fined) but not managers – unless your name is Marco Giampaolo. He watched his Serie B Brescia team lose 2-1 at home to Crotone in 2013, and then held talks with a fans' group. The following day he didn't turn up for training and his phone appeared to be switched off; the same thing occurred the next day and the day after, which meant that Brescia's assistant coaches took charge of the midweek fixture against Carpi. Unsurprisingly, the next day, the club announced that Giampaolo had left by mutual consent.

THE MYSTERY OF THE MISSING WORLD CUP STARS

The 2007 Homeless World Cup was hosted by Denmark, with no fewer than 15 players using the tournament as an opportunity to pull a fast one and try to stay in Europe. Seven men from Burundi, four from Liberia, three from Cameroon and one Afghan player disappeared after the competition, with police promising to arrest and deport any that they found. They were never caught.

THE MYSTERY OF THE SERIAL NO-SHOW ADRIANO

After heading to Brazil on international duty in April 2009, Inter Milan striker Adriano decided he quite liked it back home and refused to return to Italy. He sweated it out for almost four weeks until the Italians decided to cancel his contract. He joined Flamengo, where he scored on his debut but failed to show up for training the week after. Eventually, Roma convinced him to return to Italy but in 2011 he decided to stay in Brazil while recovering from a broken arm, much to the irritation of the Italians. A year later he was back at Flamengo but, after just two weeks, he skipped training and never played for the club again. After a year away from football, it was time for a fresh start, at Atletico Paranaense. But following the club's exit from the Copa Libertadores, Adriano did his David Copperfield routine and didn't appear at the next two training sessions before his contract was terminated.

THE MYSTERY OF THE ELUSIVE ZAKI

Wigan's on-loan Egyptian striker made a habit of being late and was fined by manager Steve Bruce for his troubles, but he went one better than tardiness after an international break in April 2009. This time, he didn't bother returning to the club at all, leading Bruce to label him 'the most unprofessional player I've ever worked with'. He didn't start another game for the Latics and, the following month, the club decided against the option of making his loan deal permanent.

THE MYSTERY OF THE MISSING SOL CAMPBELL

The Arsenal defender was playing at home to West Ham one Wednesday night, but was not his usual self. His miskick let Nigel Reo-Coker in to score for the Hammers and he was easily barged off the ball for the visitors' second as Arsenal came in at the break trailing 2-1. In the dressing room, he took off his boots and told his team-mates he couldn't go on. He was substituted, and left the ground immediately, heading straight to Brussels to stay with a friend, although he didn't tell anyone where he was. Not even Arsene Wenger. Eventually, Arsenal director David Dein got in touch and went out to Belgium to meet him. After five days off and missing a victory at Birmingham, Campbell returned to training but was to leave Arsenal at the end of the season.

THE MYSTERY OF THE SULKING YOHAN CABAYE

Frustrated at not being allowed a transfer, Newcastle's French midfielder decided that the start of the 2013/14 season was not for him. He missed Premier League games against West Ham and Manchester City and a glamour League Cup trip to Morecambe, without any explanation for his absence. He was duly fined two weeks' wages and eventually left the club the following January.

THE MYSTERY OF THE INVISIBLE ARIEL ORTEGA

The Argentine midfielder left Fenerbahce for an international match, but failed to return to the Turkish club on time. Which is an understatement, as he actually stayed away for two months and was then handed a four-month suspension for his trouble.

THE MYSTERY OF THE AWOL DIOUF

Blackburn's notoriously awkward striker El Hadji Diouf decided not to turn up for Rovers' pre-season training, or a trip to Austria before the 2011/12 season. 'I don't know where he is right now, but I know where he will be tomorrow – or at least he's telling us he'll be here on [Wednesday],' said manager Steve Kean unconvincingly at the time. 'He's not been here since the end of last season and we tried to make contact with him and couldn't.'

THE MYSTERY OF THE NEVER-PRESENT CARLOS TEVEZ

Manchester City's star striker missed training one morning in November 2011 and it was soon discovered that the player had returned to Argentina. This was during the fall-out over his alleged refusal to warm up during a Champions League tie at Bayern Munich. Tevez was so incensed that he didn't return to Manchester until February 2012, completing a rather luxurious AWOL during which time he was regularly pictured playing golf. It was particularly luxurious as City fined their player £1.2 million for refusing to come back to the UK.

The golf club thief has struck and Carlos has no idea

THE UNLIKELIEST ENGLAND PLAYERS TO PLAY FOR ENGLAND

With his gangly and unorthodox style, Carlton Palmer wasn't the most obvious England international (never mind manager). Here are some other internationals who raised the occasional eyebrow:

GEOFF THOMAS

It's probably unfair that the former Crystal Palace star will always be associated with that awful, awful miss when clean through for England against France in 1992. Thomas was about 25 yards from goal, and with the keeper approaching he had three options:

1. Go around him.
2. Chip it over him.
3. Shoot either side of him.

Thomas went for number four – scuff a howler somewhere near the corner flag. Geoff is a very nice man... that remains a very bad miss.

ANTHONY GARDNER

A promising defender at one stage in his career but when you think of Moore, Butcher and Adams, the one-time Spurs centre-back was probably not an England player.

CHRIS POWELL

It's fair to say that at the age of 31, the Charlton left-back had accepted he would never get to represent his country. But along came Sven-Goran Eriksson and handed him a belated England career.

RICKIE LAMBERT

The Saints striker received a thoroughly deserved call-up to the England 2014 World Cup squad, but few would have predicted his old-fashioned and outdated rise from beetroot-jar factory worker, prolific lower-league marksman with Stockport, Rochdale, Macclesfield and Bristol Rovers to Premier League powerhouse. Lambert's rise makes every lower league footballer dream. It's also great to see someone who looks genuinely delighted to play for his country. Lambert for prime minister.

MICHAEL BALL

Not the musical sensation who sang 'Love Changes Everything', but the Everton left-back who was another beneficiary of Sven's generosity and played one game for England before disappearing back into relative obscurity.

STEVE BULL

A superb lower-league striker, Bull has the distinction of making 13 appearances for England (including a visit to the 1990 World Cup) and scoring five goals, despite never playing top-flight football. Instead, Bull seemed to enjoy smashing pretty much every single Wolves goalscoring record.

GAVIN MCCANN

He wasn't Scottish so was eligible to wear the Three Lions, but that didn't mean he had to be picked. The Sunderland midfielder was another one-hit wonder who probably still has to convince good friends that his England cap is real.

DAVID NUGENT

A prolific goal machine at lower levels, Nugent was handed his one and only England chance while still a Championship player with Preston. He grabbed it with both, er, feet by scoring – a tap-in against San Marino which was going in anyway, thus denying Jermain Defoe a goal.

STEVE GUPPY

The lower-league journeyman worked his way up to the top flight with Leicester and duly received his England nod after impressing for the Foxes. He played one game and never received the nod again.

MICHAEL RICKETTS

In a reverse of Guppy's path, Ricketts managed to reach the top flight with Bolton quite quickly, then played for England before spending the rest of his career turning out for the likes of Oldham, Southend and Todmorden Over-35s. OK, the last one was a joke.

PETER CROUCH

To complete this rather unusual set of England players, we have possibly the most unusual footballer of all time. Tall, awkward, clumsy but incredibly talented, Crouch defied the odds by saving his best performances – and goal celebrations – for his country. It's also very annoying that despite having an excellent record for England, critics complained that he didn't score against 'big' sides. Some people can do nothing right.

I have played for England, once. A 5-0 charity match win over Wales (100 per cent record)

FOOTBALL'S GREATEST GINGER XI

Was Paul Scholes the greatest ginger footballer of all time? He's certainly up there and gives us the opportunity to put together a list of the world's (no, they're not all Scottish) ginger-est footballers.

Billy Bremner

Fiery, ferocious and Scottish, the Leeds skipper ticked all the ginger boxes.

Alexi Lalas

The American rocker used to have football's famous facial hair.

Sean Dyche

As a manager, he became the Ginger Mourinho, heroically guiding Burnley back to the Premier League.

Alan Ball

England's World Cup-winning ginger wins a place in any team, especially this one.

Matthias Sammer

The token Teuton was a powerful presence in the German midfield with a magnificent strawberry blond barnet.

Elierce Barbosa de Souza

Every team needs a gifted Brazilian – this one gets the only ginger Brazilian in the known universe.

Mark Pembridge

The former Derby, Everton and Fulham midfielder was Welsh (just in case you assumed he was a Scot).

Dave Kitson

It's no secret that the prolific lower-league striker has copper on top and his goalscoring prowess makes him a must for this side.

John Hartson

Who better to partner Kitson up front than the fiery Welshman? Brother Hartson shaves the whole lot off these days, which is hugely disappointing.

Adam Bogdan

Every team needs a goalkeeper, and the Hungarian stopper has all the credentials to make this one.

Gordon Strachan

The midfield maverick who owned the 1980s ginger look could easily be this side's player-boss. His mullet took ginger to a whole new level.

I should briefly add here that I used to play with a ginger-haired lad during my time at Sheffield University. He once got a red card while playing away at Leeds (if I remember rightly) and as he left the pitch was serenaded with a hastily arranged, rather harsh but ultimately brilliant ballad: 'Red card, red pubes, red card, red pubes'. Simple and yet strangely effective.

Ginger schoolboy

Electrical XI

During my ludicrously long wait for Carlton Palmer I tried to entertain myself on *Snake* on my old-school Nokia. Since those days the electrical entertainment industry has come on in leaps and bounds. Many techno names were suggested for the Electrical XI but only a chosen few made the cut. These are they:

Team Name: PS3 Eindhoven
Reserves: Maccabi HiFi
Stadium: Craven Wattage

Management Team
Pluggie Freedman
Mark Fuse

Chairman
Plug Ellis

First Team
Zanussi Jaaskelainen
Graeme Le Sauxing Machine
Wayne Fridge
Gary Breville
Eric Blenda Blenda
BluRay Parlour
Braun Wright-Phillips
Tumble Dyer
Peter Modemwingie
Sony Yeboah
Zlatan IbraDimmerSwitch (c)

Subs
Peter SchMicrowave
iPaddy Kenny
Nigel Delonghi
Apple Macelele
Lava Lampard

MEMORABILIA

Pele doesn't make my top three footballers. The places on the podium are reserved for Zinedine Zidane, the Brazilian Ronaldo and Chris Waddle (Michael Laudrup just misses out in fourth). Despite that, Pele is one of only two people I have ever asked for an autograph. The other was Glenn Hoddle, who completely ignored me in front of my entire class outside Gatwick airport in the mid-1990s.

I broke all the rules for Pele, though, when I was interviewing him a few years ago. I had even planned things out by taking a Brazil shirt along. The chat went really well as the legend waxed lyrical on various subjects. At the end we shook hands and I asked the great number 10 if he would sign my shirt. I explained that I never normally ask for autographs and for some reason described the Hoddle incident. He glazed over when I got to the bit about Gatwick airport but briefly came off autopilot to scribble 'All the best Dan, Pele'.

As part of the press conference I'd also managed to get my hands on a nice retro New York Cosmos bag that would be perfect for the gym. As I thanked Pele, he picked up the bag and started putting indelible marker pen to shiny green surface. 'DON'T SIGN THE BAG, PELE!' I hollered. He stopped mid-signature and the room fell silent. People started looking at each other in a disbelieving did-he-really-just-ask-Pele-not-to-sign-the-bag? fashion. Perhaps I should have explained that turning up to the gym with a bag signed by Pele would make me look like a moron, but I tried to make light of it and offered a grovelling apology. The great man laughed as he observed, 'You're the only person who has ever asked me NOT to sign something!'

We shook hands and he disappeared into a fog of publicists. The green New York Cosmos bag with 'Pe...' on it remains a treasured possession.

Unusual Football Memorabilia That Isn't a Bag Half-signed by Pele

While it's obvious that nothing will ever beat my half-signed Pele bag, there is a great deal of weird and wonderful footballing memorabilia out there. We've narrowed it down to the best (or worst) that give my Pele bag a run for its money.

Arsenal Russian dolls found in Prague (l to r: Fabregas, Van Persie, Lehmann, Rosicky, Gallas).

Burton Albion v Manchester United, FA Cup third round 2005, commemorative Bovril (also available in red for United fans).

The Hannover 96 Toaster – no home is complete without one (also available in Dortmund, Hertha Berlin and St Pauli).

Who wouldn't want a ceramic likeness of Sergio Ramos going to the toilet?

A must for any Liverpool fan, this Everton club crest says Liverpool FC so it must be genuine, right?

If you're a fan of Fulham, Mohamed Al-Fayed and Michael Jackson, you can't go wrong with this t-shirt, complete with unique club crest.

Apparently, you can even get turned away from some of the worst bars in Liverpool wearing this horrific 'Anfield' shirt on a night out.

Give him what he wants for Christmas: Newcastle United flashing antlers.

Arguably the rarest tattoo ever, mainly because this Manchester City fan jumped the gun ever so slightly...

Souvenir bags aside, the New York Cosmos were once football's most fashionable club as the stars flocked to play for them. But they weren't the only ones about whom it became achingly trendy to wax lyrical over the years. Here are a few more candidates...

FC ST PAULI
The German 'punk' team have long been hailed as an example of how a club should be run, with politically left-leaning fans creating vibrant atmospheres at every home game, hours before the match has even started. Some of the infectious St Pauli chants have made it over to British football to underline the club's growing influence.

BORUSSIA DORTMUND AND JURGEN KLOPP
The club was already cool in the eyes of many Teuton-philes who admired BvB and Klopp's footballing philosophy of playing the 'right way'. Then came the glorious run to the 2013 Champions League final and the world fell in love with the Germans, especially Klopp, who delivered lines like this: 'Shinji Kagawa is one of the best players in the world and he now plays twenty minutes at Manchester United – on the left wing! My heart breaks. Really, I have tears in my eyes.' Klopp is also the only person I have ever interviewed who used the word 'Boom!' mid-chat and didn't sound like an idiot.

FRANCE 1982 WORLD CUP TEAM

After the travesty of their semi-final defeat at the hands of West Germany and goalkeeper Harald Schumacher, the French became much loved and idolised. Led by Michel Platini, and with others like Didier Six and Dominique Rocheteau in their side, they went on to win Euro 1984 to the delight of Europe.

FULHAM

When Mohamed Al-Fayed's money started bankrolling Fulham through the divisions and inexorably towards the Premier League, the stars began to flock to Craven Cottage, most notably Michael Jackson. Even Liz Hurley and Lily Allen became fans. Al-Fayed also offered plenty of proof for the age-old truth that if you give a man too much money he just buys the most expensive clothes rather than anything that actually matches.

CHELSEA

Continuing the west London theme, pre-Abramovich Chelsea made plenty of football fans go weak at the knees when Ruud Gullit brought his 'sheckshi' football to Stamford Bridge. Even Dennis Wise became an amiable type of guy.

BRAZIL

Before you read this, try to wipe the 7-1 mullering at the 2014 World Cup from your mind. Done it? On you go... When have Brazil not been the most fashionable football team in the world? From the always-trendy yellow shirts (especially the 1970 edition which never ages) to the samba skills and the five World Cups, the South Americans are invariably the biggest draw in world football. Makes you sick, doesn't it?

AJAX

Their academy sends their young players to school alongside football training; their philosophy is to get the ball down and pass; they've won a few European Cups playing Total Football and they even get old stars back to work at the club. What's not to like?

JOSE MOURINHO

He may have lost a little of his sparkle but there was a time when we were all hooked. The suits, the arrogance, the charm, the looks – The Special One may be the ultimate wind-up merchant but he did everything with style and was undeniably successful too.

LAURIE CUNNINGHAM

One of the sharpest-dressed footballers in the 1970s, Cunningham broke down boundaries as a young, black footballer who went from Orient to Real Madrid via West Brom in the blink of an eye. His extraordinary talent on the pitch was matched by his super-cool demeanour off it. His sadly premature death only served to enhance his cult status.

GEORGE BEST

The first celebrity footballer managed to remain cool even when his life was spiralling out of control. Best was a hipster, the man about town who paved the way for the wannabe football playboys and prima donnas who would follow years later. Very few will ever match his effort-less talent.

The late, great and Best

FORGOTTEN FOOTBALL TEAMS

The New York Cosmos came and went – and then came again – but plenty of clubs were not so lucky as they disappeared forever. But were they ever really there?

JOSSY'S GIANTS

The kids' team shot to fame in the 1980s thanks to their links with former footballer Jossy Blair, but vanished without a trace soon after. Twenty man points if you are able to sing the theme tune to these lyrics:

> *Here go Jossy's Giants,*
> *Football's just a branch of science,*
> *Head the ball, now Jossy calls...*
> *Jossy's Giants!*

Sid Waddell did a lot of things well but this must be among his finest work.

WALFORD TOWN

In the glory days, Arthur Fowler had a season ticket and the team seemed to be set for the big time. But Arthur's sad death in 1996 coincided with the club's demise.

MELCHESTER ROVERS

Despite an astonishing 42-trophy haul in the glory days of the 1960s, 70s and 80s, Melchester have not played a competitive game since 2001.

HARCHESTER UNITED

So successful in the 1990s, they were a weekly fixture on Sky, but the club soon fell on hard times and were never heard of again.

EARLS PARK FC

The club took the Premier League by storm between 2002 and 2006, with rarely a day going by when it didn't feature on the front or back pages. But that was mainly due to the exploits of its *Footballers' Wives* rather than any on-field achievements. Once WAG-mania dipped, Earls Park were consigned to oblivion.

THE MANAGERESS FC

The top-flight club that was known only by the name 'us' or 'we' stole the headlines back in 1989 by appointing British football's first female coach. But, despite her Italian roots, Cherie Lunghi couldn't inspire her team to stick around for more than a couple of seasons.

ALLIED PRISONERS OF WAR XI

They played one memorable match in 1981, when they came from 4-1 down to claim a 4-4 draw with a team of German soldiers, but that proved to be their only game. Perhaps they couldn't afford to pay the likes of Pele, Bobby Moore and Ossie Ardiles every week.

Pele gives Sly some bad goalkeeping coaching

CARRYING TOO MUCH TIMBER

I put the Brazilian Ronaldo in my top three best players, although I'm sure he would struggle these days after piling on a fair amount of weight just before and after his retirement. And he's not the only player or ex-player to have suffered with weight problems.

Paul Gascoigne

You don't get Mars bars thrown at you if you're a picture of health and fitness. Gazza struggled with his weight throughout his career, but covered it up by pulling on his fake plastic breasts.

Mick Quinn

A prolific goalscorer who didn't let his lardiness stop him from achieving greatness. As his adoring fans used to sing: 'He's fat, he's round, he's worth a million pounds, Micky Quinn, Micky Quinn!'

Neville Southall

Southall never really got the recognition his skills deserved and perhaps some of that was down to the fact that he looked like he ate a team-mate after every game. There was no doubting his quality. Rumour has it his cap once came off in an FA Cup match and he caught it in one hand and saved the shot with the other. I also played against him in a charity match at Pride Park a few seasons ago and – even though he has continued to eat team-mates since retirement – the quality was still there in spades.

William 'Fatty' Foulke

The 1902 FA Cup-winning Sheffield United goalkeeper was renowned for his considerable weight, with reports suggesting he tipped the scales at 24 stone. It's also thought that the chant 'Who ate all the pies' was first directed at him all those years ago.

Jamie Pollock

The former Middlesbrough and Manchester City midfielder didn't hold back after his early retirement at the age of 28. And when I say hold back, I mean it looks like he hasn't skipped a meal since.

Neil Shipperley

The nippy striker was predatory for Crystal Palace, Barnsley and Wimbledon back in his day. But it seems he maintained his predatory instincts at mealtimes as his move into non-League management coincided with him ballooning beyond recognition and the papers dubbing him Neil Chipperley. Harsh... very harsh.

Neil Shipperley in leaner days

Jan Molby

The former Liverpool star battled with his weight throughout his career, coming in at more than 14 stone, but that didn't stop him enjoying success, racking up so many trophies that Liverpool fans would quip that he was worth his weight in gold.

Kevin Pressman

The Sheffield Wednesday goalkeeper suffered jibes about his weight every time he stood in the net in front of opposition fans. And it was probably justified given that he was more than 15 stone. Pressman is also responsible for the best penalty ever taken, during an FA Cup replay against Wolves in February 1995. It is well worth a visit to YouTube. Pressman smashed the ball with so much force it would have rendered a rhinoceros unconscious. It remains perhaps the most 'unsaveable' spot-kick in the history of this planet of ours.

Andy Reid

The Republic of Ireland international was known as the 'Fat Maradona', which tells you pretty much everything you need to know.

CLOTHING XI

The Pele shirt remains a permanent fixture on the office wall but perhaps Pele's only career regret is that he never made it into the Clothing XI. Here are those who did:

Team Name: The Kaizer Briefs
Reserves: Borussia MonchenSlingBacks
Stadium: Stadium Of Tights

Management Team
Roberto Mankini & Leotardo

First Team
Fruit Of The Poom
Skrtleneck
Dickson Etutu
Chino Flores
Younes Kagoule
Nigel De Thong
Carlos ValderUnderArma
SkinnyJeans Zidane (c)
Poncho Shelvey
Peter OdemStringyVest
Ji Dong Wonsie

Subs
Edwin Van Der Sari
Pat Jeggins
Tweed Malbranque
BurKaka
Dunga-rees
Snood Van Nistelrooy

My first job in football was to get a croissant for Ken Monkou. I was doing work experience at Soccer AM and Mr Monkou came in a hungry man. I took things up a notch and bought him two croissants and a collection of jams. He looked at me as if to say, 'How did you know I was a double-dough-based-product kind of man?' Task number one had been a roaring success.

My first meeting with Brian Clough was equally memorable. My role was to collect him from the car park with an ITV producer called Don. The car arrived and the door opened. Don introduced us both:

'Mr Clough... I'm Don and this is Dan. We are both looking after you today. Anything you need, just let us know.'

Clough looked at us with a wry smile and burst forth. 'Listen, sons. I think you'll find that your mother called you Donald [pointing at Don] and you Daniel [finger in my direction] and that's what I shall call you. Now, which one of you makes the best cup of tea?'

Ken's croissant and Clough are all well and good, but I often get asked about my most embarrassing moments. The time when things go horribly wrong, the *You've Been Framed!* classic when a horse bites your neck on live TV or a small child volleys a ball unintentionally into your nether regions.

I did nearly get killed by Tidal Bay at the Grand National but I shall save that tale for another day. Far and away the most embarrassing incident I can remember occurred in the presence of Jordan... in this case the supermodel who was once married to Peter Andre.

When I first started working in radio at Key103 in Manchester I used to have to straddle the departments of both news and sport. I did my best to fill my days with football but occasionally I had to work for the dark side. The local Manchester elections were one such occasion – when Jordan was running for the seat in Stretford and Urmston as part of a publicity stunt for a national newspaper.

My editor at the time, the great John Pickford, sent me down to the leisure centre where all the candidates were gathered on results night with the classic sentence ringing in my ears:

'If you don't come back with an interview with that model then don't bother coming back.'

I seem to remember a grand total of three people voted for her that night, all of whom turned up with semi-naked pictures to be signed and two of whom were uncontrollably drunk. Beverley Hughes won the seat but as soon as the result was announced Jordan and her posse left the hall en masse.

As they cantered down the corridor they were flanked by TV crews and photographers. I jogged alongside and managed to wedge myself into the perfect position.

'Will you be back to fight for the seat again?' I asked her, shoving my microphone underneath her nose. Unfortunately, I had neglected to spot the awkwardly placed wheelie bin and just as she started to answer the question I hit it at a fast enough speed to go over the top of it, enter it briefly, spill its contents on my face and exit (post-tumble) with the recording equipment intact and enough balance to collect the rest of her answer on my return to the upright position.

At the time I felt that I'd managed to 'style out' an otherwise painfully awkward situation. The fact that a section of banana skin was removed from my cranium upon my return to the newsroom would suggest the opposite.

TEN BRIAN CLOUGH CLASSICS

It was an honour and a privilege to be taken to task by Cloughie in my early days at Granada, but he saved his best lines for bigger footballing fish than me. Here are some classic Cloughisms:

1. ON ROME
'Rome wasn't built in a day, but then again I wasn't on that particular job.'

2. ON RESOLVING PLAYER DISAGREEMENTS
'We talk about it for twenty minutes and then we decide I was right.'

3. ON DAVID SEAMAN
'David Seaman is a handsome young man but he spends too much time looking in his mirror rather than at the ball. You can't keep goal with hair like that.'

4. ON LONG-BALL FOOTBALL
'If God had wanted us to play football in the clouds, he'd have put grass up there.'

5. ON SVEN-GORAN ERIKSSON GETTING THE ENGLAND JOB
'At last we've appointed a manager who speaks English better than the players.'

6. ON MANCHESTER UNITED'S DECISION TO MISS THE FA CUP TO PLAY IN THE 1999 WORLD CLUB CHAMPIONSHIP
'United in Brazil? I hope they all get bloody diarrhoea.'

7. ON THE ADJUSTMENT TO THE OFFSIDE RULE

'If any one of my players isn't interfering with play, they're not getting paid.'

8. TO THE NOTTINGHAM FOREST PHYSIO AFTER STUART PEARCE SUFFERED CONCUSSION IN AN FA CUP TIE

'Tell him he's Pele and that he's playing up front for the last ten minutes.'

9. TO MARTIN O'NEILL AFTER HE'D ASKED WHY HE'D BEEN DROPPED

'Because you're too good for the first team.'

10. ON HIS STANDING IN THE GAME

'I wouldn't say I was the best manager in the business... but I was in the top one.'

Cloughie was a big fan of the old buzzer-in-the-hand gag

Brazilian One-named Wonders

Thinking of the singularly titled Jordan also makes you think of the many Brazilian footballers who became known by a single moniker. But what happened to their surnames and how did they get their nicknames?

Pele

Where else could we start? Edson Arantes do Nascimento just doesn't have the same ring to it as Pele. He was named Edson after the American inventor Thomas Edison, with his parents deciding the 'i' was unnecessary. Nobody really knows where the Pele name comes from. The most likely explanation is that an Irish priest who saw him play used the Gaelic words *'Ag imirt peile'*, which means 'playing football', and kids repeated the last word, believing that it was Edson's name. And it seems to have stuck.

A perfect example of a powerful man-shake with Edson

Kaka

If it wasn't for Kaka's younger brother Rodrigo, we'd all be calling him Ricardo, which is his real name – or Ricardo Izecson dos Santos Leite, to be accurate. But Rodrigo found it tough to say Ricardo and, as a result, Ricardo became known as Kaka, which was all that his kid brother could manage. My brother called me 'Dump Head' for at least three years. Thankfully it never caught on.

Hulk

The burly striker was born Givanildo Vieira de Souza which wouldn't be anywhere near as much fun as being named after a cult TV character. And that's exactly what Givanildo's father thought as well, as he was a huge fan of the series so decided to nickname his son accordingly. Inevitable headlines followed when Hulk made it as a pro, best of all when he was banned for four months in Portugal following a tunnel brawl, when he was labelled 'The Ineligible Hulk'.

Socrates

The exception to the rule, as Socrates wasn't actually nicknamed at all – this was his real name: Socrates Brasileiro Sampaio de Souza Vieira de Oliveira. But the headband and beard, not to mention the football, meant that he couldn't be overlooked.

Zico

Arthur Antunes Coimbra was one of the greatest midfielders in history but probably wouldn't have been all that if he'd been known as Arthur. Luckily, the baby of the family used to be called Arthurzinho in an affectionate way, which quickly became Arthurzico, and then just Zico. Don't you just love Brazilians?

Careca

The man born as Antonio de Oliveira Filho was fairly keen on a famous Brazilian clown when he was a child, so much so that the name of that clown became his nickname through two World Cups. For the record, Careca actually means 'bald'.

Bebeto

The player who shot to fame by pretending to rock his new-born baby after scoring in the 1994 World Cup quarter-final v Holland has his own explanation of how he became known by his nickname, instead of Jose Roberto Gama de Oliveira. 'Most Robertos are labelled Beto,' he explains. 'Well, as a kid, I was originally Beto as well. But as I always scored the most goals in the games we played in the streets, it became Bebeto. Always double.'

Dunga

Bebeto's fellow 1994 World Cup winner was originally Carlos Caetano Bledorn Verri, but an uncle – who must have been a big Disney fan – nicknamed him Dunga, which is the Portuguese translation of the dwarf named Dopey in the *Snow White* film. He could have chosen any of the seven as it was Dunga's lack of height as a kid, rather than intelligence, that was the reference point. But he chose Dopey nonetheless. Cheers, Unc.

Garrincha

The double World Cup-winning legend was named by his sister due to his frail size as a four-year-old. Manuel Francisco dos Santos was smaller than other kids his age so his sibling Rosa began calling him Garrincha, which means 'little bird' or 'wren' in that part of Brazil.

Funny Football Oneliners

Cloughie wasn't the only football man with a sense of humour, as proved by this little collection of memorable quips from the beautiful game.

Interviewer to Peter Crouch: 'What would you have been if you weren't a footballer?' Crouch: 'A virgin.'

George Best: 'I spent a lot of my money on booze, birds and fast cars – the rest I just squandered.'

Ian Holloway, after QPR beat Cardiff: 'I couldn't be more chuffed if I were a badger in mating season.'

Bill Shankly: 'Of course I didn't take my wife to see Rochdale as an anniversary present. It was her birthday. Would I have got married in the football season? Anyway, it was Rochdale reserves.'

Terry Venables: 'I had mixed feelings – like watching my mother-in-law drive over a cliff in your car.'

Nat Lofthouse: 'There were plenty of players in the fifties who would kick your b******s off. At the end they would shake your hand and help you look for them.'

Harry Redknapp on Iain Dowie: 'Judging by the shape of his face, he must have headed a lot of goals.'

Millwall manager Mark McGhee on rumours his player Marc Bircham was being linked with Tottenham: 'The only way Marc Bircham will be going to Tottenham is if he buys a season ticket.'

Ron Atkinson on Gordon Strachan: 'There's nobody fitter at his age – except maybe Raquel Welch.'

Jason McAteer on Roy Keane's autobiography: 'I call it the *Satanic Verses*.'

Ryan Giggs on Dennis Wise: 'If he fouls you he normally picks you up but the referee doesn't see what he picks you up by.'

Tommy Docherty: 'The Liverpool theme tune is "You'll Never Walk Alone", the Wimbledon one is "You'll Never Walk Again".'

THE BEST (AND WORST) FOOTBALL PUBLICITY STUNTS

Jordan's election campaign was one of many famous political publicity stunts we've seen over the years, which got me pondering some of the most brilliant examples of football publicity stunts. This way please...

DUTCH BEER AMBUSH I

The 2010 World Cup match between Holland and Denmark was memorable for one reason – and it wasn't the Dutch team's 2-0 win. Instead, TV cameras kept focusing on 36 attractive young Dutchwomen, all dressed in orange miniskirts, the outfit that is associated with Bavaria beer. This so appalled FIFA, whose official beer sponsor Budweiser pays fortunes for that very title, that all the women were ordered out of the stadium. But the ploy had worked as images of the Bavaria beer girls were instantly flashed across world media.

DUTCH BEER AMBUSH II

Bavaria were no strangers to a World Cup marketing ambush, as they'd shown in 2006 in Germany, albeit not quite as successfully. On this occasion, dozens of male Dutch fans were ordered to remove their orange lederhosen featuring the beer's name, which meant they were forced to watch in their underpants as their side beat Ivory Coast.

MESSI BACKFIRES

One attempt at publicity which didn't go according to plan featured Lionel Messi, who was supposed to appear as a substitute in a game at Hackney Marshes. He was flown in by helicopter, but there was pandemonium as hundreds of fans flocked to see him, and his appearance was cancelled for safety reasons.

THE GRIM REAPER

Just when you thought that our bookie friends couldn't milk any more out of football, they sent an Everton 'fan' dressed as the Grim Reaper to sit right behind beleaguered Manchester United manager David Moyes at Goodison Park in 2014, a game that turned out to be Moyes's last in charge. The Grim Reaper – with a bookies' branded scythe and cloak – was removed from the ground during the game, but not before pictures had been taken and circulated in the usual manner. Job done.

WE ARE ALL MONKEYS

When Barcelona's Dani Alves chomped on a banana thrown by a racist Villarreal fan before taking a corner, a worldwide outpouring of support followed on social media, with other footballers, and thousands of people, sending pictures of themselves eating bananas. But the genius stunt was dreamed up by Brazilian marketing agency Loducca. They planned that the next time Neymar or his team-mate had a banana thrown at them, they should eat it. And once that happened, the campaign was ready to go live. Neymar tweeted his support with a picture of himself eating a banana alongside his son and a toy banana, with the message: 'We are all monkeys, we are all the same. Say no to racism.' Neymar's 10 million followers made sure that tweet went viral and, before long, the t-shirts were printed and a worldwide victory for anti-racism was being celebrated.

BAYERN MUNICH'S NEW SIGNING

At about 1pm one day in 2013, Bayern Munich revealed to its 2.7 million Facebook fans that a major announcement would be made in an hour about the signing of a new offensive player. Fans, journalists and millions more rushed to the club's Facebook page, eagerly awaiting the news as speculation reached frenzied levels. Then, an hour later, a recorded-as-live press conference featuring the club's communications chief, general manager and Philipp Lahm announced that: 'The new star player is... YOU – the twelfth man of the squad.' A series of videos followed with players reacting to the 'news' with delight, which was, unsurprisingly, the completely opposite reaction of the club's fans who complained bitterly about being duped.

CANTONA FOR PRESIDENT

The Frenchman fooled a Paris newspaper – and many international outlets – by telling them he was out collecting the signatures of 500 elected officials to gain their support in his bid to challenge Nicolas Sarkozy for the French presidency. The news spread like wildfire to general disbelief, which was backed up when it emerged that Cantona had been working with a housing charity and was actually canvassing signatures for a petition asking for more funds to solve the nation's homeless problem. Sarkozy's sigh of relief could be heard as far away as London. Probably.

BENDTNER'S BRIEFS

When Denmark's Nicklas Bendtner scored his second goal of the Euro 2012 game against Portugal, he celebrated by lowering his shorts to reveal a pair of green pants bearing the name of bookmaker Paddy Power. UEFA didn't find it funny and fined the striker 100,000 euros, and banned him for a game for good measure. Naturally, the bookies offered to pay the fine – but not play the next game for him.

European XI

Many of the stars we've mentioned in this book have come to play in England from far-flung corners of the continent of Europe. Most of them have brought flavour and colour to our football but there are some things from the mainland that we just shouldn't celebrate: French public toilets and Eurovision. They both make you feel a little dirty. I believe it was during one particularly dull night of Eurovision that the finest punners in the land were called upon to lighten proceedings with a European XI.

Team Name: Partizan Downgrade
Stadium: Liberté Égalité Fraternité

Management Team
Sir Alps Ramsey
Malta Smith

First Team
Isle Of Manninger
Channel Crossingwa
Charles N'Bosnia
Treaty Of Desailly (c)
Kris Commons Agricultural Policy
Spain Routledge
FaGreece Muamba
Leaning Tower Of Pienaar
IstanBullard
Lomana Loire Loire Valley
Venice Bergkamp

Subs
Gareth Bale Out
Stephane ReSessegnon   IceLandon Donovan
Euro Djorkaeff   Sweden Hazard

MUSIC AND FOOTBALL

WHEN MARIO MET NOEL

There are certain things that go very well together – tuna and mayonnaise, rhubarb and custard, milkshake and chips (try it before you turn your nose up) and music and football.

Every dressing room has someone in charge of the 'tunes', every team has a player who isn't ever allowed to select the music and almost every band includes a die-hard supporter (normally the drummer).

A few years ago we used to see Vinnie Jones walking into grounds carrying a ghetto blaster the size of a large dog but these days no 'team arrival shot' is complete without at least half the players resplendent in massive headphones. According to OPTA (the statistic you are about to read is entirely fabricated) at least 27 per cent of post-match interviews are conducted with aforementioned headphones draped around the neck ready to be replaced within 1.2 seconds of the words 'thanks for your time' being uttered.

There is, however, some good to be juiced from this situation. The footballers who want to be musicians and musicians who long to walk in the footsteps of footballers are always quite keen on a collaboration. Over the past few years I've been able to gently massage a few of those high-profile relationships to make some nice telly. Sometimes a rock 'n' roll star can open doors that remain firmly shut to lesser humans.

'Hi, Mario, I'm Dan Walker.'

'Hello,' said Balotelli, extending his hand before quickly withdrawing it. 'Wait... BBC? Journalist?'

'Yes.'

'I do not like you already.'

That was the conversation that accompanied my first meeting with Mr Balotelli, the Italian forward who has now sadly left Manchester City after providing media outlets with hours of footage.

I'd been waiting for Mario with Noel Gallagher at Manchester City's training ground. We arrived nice and early and had been shown around by Patrick Vieira, who is near the top of my 'finest Frenchmen I've met' list – just behind the guy who gave me an extra 'boule' of chocolate ice cream in the summer of 2012.

The chat with Balotelli had taken months to set up. Despite spending so much time in the UK papers during his spell here, for everything from dressing up as Santa Claus and handing out money in Manchester to an impromptu firework display in his bathroom, Balotelli has no time for the media.

Like every other broadcaster, I'd had various interview requests turned down so I approached Manchester City with the idea of getting lifelong fan, and Balotelli obsessive, Noel Gallagher, to ask the questions. 'Let me talk to Mario' was the furthest negotiations had ever progressed before, and my excitement was justified when a week later we got: 'He'll do it. He likes Oasis and he'll talk to Noel... but only Noel.'

My evil plan was hatching. All I needed now was to persuade a man in the middle of a world tour to change his itinerary to fit in an interview with a footballer. Cue two weeks of conversations with agents, agencies, friends, milkmen and friends of friends to find a suitable date and a suitable location. The good news was that, when I eventually got to Noel, he said yes immediately and changed his diary within about ten minutes.

You can still watch the interview on the wonderweb somewhere and it remains the only one Balotelli did during his time in England and the longest we've ever run on *Football Focus* in the 40-plus-year history of the show. The most telling moment for me was right at the end when Noel asked Mario if he had any questions for him, and Balotelli simply asked with an admirable innocence and slight degree of bewilderment, 'Why do you like me so much?'

Noel laughed and responded beautifully: 'Look at you... you're Mario Balotelli and you score goals with your shoulder. I'm a rock star but you're a megastar. As far as I'm concerned, the rest of the world can do one.'

A statement that perfectly summarises the reason why music and football are such comfortable companions.

Footballers Who
Hero-worship Musicians

Noel Gallagher was certainly in awe of Balotelli, but there are plenty of footballers who send the love in the other direction and have something of a soft spot for their musical heroes...

Jermain Defoe and Drake

'When I met Drake I was like a little kid with him because I love and appreciate his music,' said Defoe. He underlined his affection by moving from Tottenham to play in the MLS for the rapper's hometown team Toronto FC – a move which was sealed with a phone call from Drake, who gave the city the 'big sell' and also promised to show Defoe around town.

Wayne Rooney and the Stereophonics

'Just Enough Education to Perform' reads the tattoo on the England striker's forearm. There is a joke often made here about Wayne's IQ but it's also the title of his favourite Welsh rockers' 2001 best-selling album. They did once buy him a Leeds shirt with 'Rooney' on the back, which momentarily soured relations, but they also played at his wedding.

Marcus Hahnemann and Tool

The American goalkeeper is a huge heavy-metal fan, with noisemakers Tool (perhaps the greatest name in music) at the top of his charts. 'During the World Cup in Germany I had the chance to meet Tool, who are my favourite band of all time,' he told *Kerrang!* 'Kasey Keller and I went backstage at their show and I'm still really good friends with Justin [Chancellor, Tool bassist] to this day.'

Steven Gerrard and Phil Collins

The ultimate devotion to your idols is being prepared to fight for them and the Liverpool midfielder did just that when a DJ refused to play Phil Collins' *Greatest Hits* on Stevie G's birthday night out. Against all odds, when the England captain's request was turned down a major fight broke out which led to a court case in which a jacket was certainly required for Gerrard.

Pat Nevin and the Cocteau Twins

The Chelsea and Scotland star is a passionate music fan with The Fall and Joy Division among his favourite bands. But pride of place in the Nevin CD tower must go to the Cocteau Twins. There is a legend that Mr Nevin once asked to be subbed to get to a gig. I checked the tale with him during a recent radio show. He explains: 'It happened during a first-team pre-season friendly for Chelsea at Brentford. I agreed to sign a new contract if I could leg it at half time to go to the gig. It is a true story, sadly, but I did do voluntary extra training the next day to make up for it.' Training or not, Patrick, that is devotion.

Leighton Baines and Alex Turner

The full-back is a big indie fan and struck up a friendship with Miles Kane after the pair met at a wrestling event. But it's the Arctic Monkeys frontman who *really* makes Baines go weak in the knee area. The defender describes his meeting with Turner as 'a bit mad because he's a total hero'.

Andy Cole and Jodeci

Cole and who? You didn't miss much, but Cole's son will forever be tainted with the moniker given to him by his goal-crazy father. It turns out that Cole was also crazy about R&B group Jodeci and named his son Devante after the band's singer.

Stuart Pearce and Stiff Little Fingers

The Belfast 1970s punk band are the former England full-back's favourites, but he is a loyal fan of the entire genre. Pearce always liked to listen to The Clash's 'White Riot' before kick-off, and even went on to be quoted on notes of the band's singles box set: 'Back then I didn't want to hear any slow songs or any ballads; I just wanted something fast and loud that I could sing along to and jump up and down on the bed with a baseball bat like a complete idiot.' All of a sudden his Euro 96 penalty celebration seems a tad reserved.

Joey Barton and Morrissey

The pair met at Glastonbury – the controversial midfielder is a huge fan of the equally controversial singer. Barton, whose favourite song is The Smiths' 'Still Ill', received a phone call from Morrissey's minder: 'He said Moz would like to meet me – I thought it was a wind-up initially, but we set it up and because I was going to Glastonbury anyway they asked me if I wanted to watch him from the stage. I was like "Do you even have to ask?". It was brilliant.'

Terry Butcher and Iron Maiden

If you were asked to name the clubs Terry Butcher played for you'd probably say England, Ipswich and Rangers but you wouldn't dream of saying Iron Maiden. Yet the blood-stained centre-half has turned out for the band's football team and is a good pal of founder member Steve Harris. 'You have to wonder where we'd all be without them,' says Butcher of the band. Most of us would be fine, Terry!

THE FOOTBALL RECORDS YOU'VE PROBABLY NEVER HEARD OF

Sometimes, the relationship between music and football can blur, especially with all those World Cup and FA Cup final songs we all know and love. But there have also been some rare gems committed to vinyl by footballers which may just have slipped under the radar. No longer...

CLINT DEMPSEY – 'DON'T TREAD'

In 2006, the American teamed up with rapper Big Hawk to record a single promoting 'soccer' in the US. Dempsey wasn't named on the track; it was his rap alter ego 'Deuce'. Lyrics included:

> *'Cause I got on my job,*
> *and made the game ferocious,*
> *I was born with a drive,*
> *I got that from no coaches*

ANDY (ANDREW) COLE – 'OUTSTANDING'

Looking for the ultimate sound of summer with a cool R&B vibe? Forget about DJ Jazzy Jeff & The Fresh Prince's timeless classic 'Summertime' and try a bit of Andy Cole's 'Outstanding'. The Manchester United striker's biggest success of 1999 wasn't his club's memorable treble, but his UK chart position of No. 68 with his debut single. The lyrics deserved so much more:

> *United forever*
> *Whatever the weather*
> *Less than a hundred per cent?*
> *Never!*

Andrew's debut single remains his only single thus far.

IGOR STIMAC – 'MARE I KATE'

The former Derby, West Ham and Hajduk Split centre-back was a no-nonsense defender who also won 52 caps for his country Croatia and went on to become their manager too. But all that is put in the shade by Stimac's collaboration with Croat band The Bohems to record *Mare I Kate* which was No. 1 in Croatia for four (FOUR) months.

MORTEN GAMST PEDERSEN – 'THIS IS FOR REAL'

Before One Direction, there was The Players. A Norwegian boy band made up of footballers, one of whom was the future Blackburn star. They released a single in 2006 to raise money for Red Cross initiative Soccer Against Crime. Talking of crimes, here are the opening lines to the song:

I swear from the first time I saw you I knew,
Yeah I swear,
Had a feeling that you could take my dreams
And make them all come true

CARLOS TEVEZ AND PIOLA VAGO

The former Manchester City, Manchester United and West Ham forward is infamous for his controversial moves, but there are none more offensive than those he performs with his band Piola Vago. The shanty town 'Cumbia' dance band features Carlos, his brother Diego and a few of their mates. Rumours that Carlos was switching to a rival shanty town five-piece have so far proved unfounded.

BMD – 'MIDAS TOUCH'

The B is for Benni McCarthy, M is Mario Melchiot while the D is supplied by their Ajax team-mate Dean Gorre. McCarthy was no stranger to chart success after his big hit 'Shibobe' with South African rapper TKZee, but it was Gorre who provided the vocals for this 1998 track. 'It was a rap/R&B record,' says Melchiot. 'Very swingy, very easy on the ears.' We'll be the judge of that, Mario.

JAY DEMERIT – 'SOCCER ROCKS'

Watford's finest American export recorded this song with his friends in Wisconsin one summer, and decided to release it as a charity single for Cancer Research. Which is all lovely, unlike these sample lyrics:

I hear my team-mates calling me
and opponents fearing a slide tackle when I have the ball
(Soccer Rocks!)

SLAVEN BILIC – 'FIERY MADNESS'

Imagine Fabio Capello, Sven-Goran Eriksson or even Roy Hodgson writing and recording an England World Cup or Euros song. It probably makes a little bit of sick come into your mouth. Yet that's what Croatia coach Slaven Bilic did for his country in Euro 2008 with his group Rawbau, for whom he's the rhythm guitarist. The song soared to No. 1.

RUUD GULLIT – 'NOT THE DANCING KIND'

The irony of this song title is that Mr Sexy Football very much *was* the dancing kind as proved by this reggae track he recorded back in 1984 when he was a Feyenoord player. The sleeve for the 7" single inexplicably showed Ruud posing in the shower, while the single equally inexplicably included these lines:

Say, all you people there
Are there some of you of the dancing kind? (Yeah!)
I said: are there some of you of the dancing kind? (Yeah!)

PELE – 'MY WORLD IS A BALL'

In many ways, everyone's world is a ball, but seeing as he's the internationally accepted greatest player ever, Pele's world is probably more of a ball than anyone else's. When he was a New York Cosmos player, Pele recorded this number with legendary Brazilian musician Sergio Mendes.

BASILE BOLI AND CHRIS WADDLE – 'WE'VE GOT A FEELING'

Everyone knows about Waddle's 'Diamond Lights' collaboration with (Glenn) Hoddle, but four years later he was at it again, this time with his Marseille team-mate. The single was released to help promote an anti-racism campaign in France, and Waddle recently claimed it topped the Albanian charts. No one has been able to verify this. What is certain, however, is that the Geordie's English lyrics were pronounced with a little French tinge, making him sound like a cross between the policeman from 'Allo 'Allo! and Schteve McClaren.

KEVIN KEEGAN – 'ENGLAND'

After a spell in Hamburg, Keegan returned to England to play for Southampton and released a follow-up single to his hit 'Head Over Heels in Love', which reached No. 10 in Germany. Unfortunately, his adoring German public were not so keen on a song in which King Kev banged on about how happy he was to be back in England, and it vanished without a trace.

VINNIE JONES AND THE SOUL SURVIVORS – 'WOOLY BULLY'

In the early 1990s, the idea that Vinnie Jones would become a Hollywood star would've been laughable – in fact, it still is. But his 1993 cover version of 'Wooly Bully' with the Soul Survivors perhaps gave an indication of what lay ahead for football's hard man, with the biggest surprise being it's not even that bad.

TOMAS BROLIN AND FRIENDS IN NEED – 'ALL OF US'

As if Brolin hadn't endured enough verbals for the 'timber' he carries around, he left another open goal for his critics with his role in a single released by 'supergroup' Friends in Need, made up of Bjorn Borg, Dr Alban, tennis coach Mattias Frisk and the Swedish footballer. It made the Swedish Top 20 but the video was banned from TV as it featured 'too many breast implants and too few clothes'. Fortunately, none of that had anything to do with Tomas.

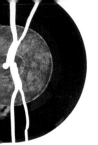

WHEN FOOTBALL AND MUSIC GO WRONG

The beautiful synergy between Balotelli and Gallagher is not always the case when the two worlds of music and football collide accidentally. Far from it, in fact.

DIANA ROSS AT USA 94

Take one massively successful pop diva and one completely unmissable penalty and you have the perfect ingredients for one of the most repeated clips in football history. The opening ceremony of USA 94 – and indeed of anything ever – will always be associated with Miss Ross's lamentably awful spot-kick. Apparently, after watching it, Chris Waddle smiled for the first time in four years.

PHIL BROWN AT THE KC STADIUM

The Beach Boys are one of the finest examples of harmonious singing in music history. Which is exactly why Hull manager Phil Brown shouldn't have attempted a rendition of Tigers' fans chant 'Don't wanna go home' to the tune of 'Sloop John B' (more about that later). When thousands sing it together, it sounds fine, but Brown holding a microphone in the middle of the pitch on his own was always going to end horribly.

PAUL MCCARTNEY AT VANCOUVER'S BC PLACE

Macca was doing his thing, belting out 'Live and Let Die' at the home of MLS outfit Vancouver Whitecaps. As usual, the pyrotechnics went off behind him, but nobody had bothered to work out that the new stadium's £300 million retractable roof was actually shut, meaning part of the tiling was burned by the fireworks.

HARPER GRUZINS IN DALLAS

Every US-based MLS game begins with a performance of the 'Star-spangled Banner' – this is America, after all. But, in possibly the biggest outrage in Dallas since John F. Kennedy's ill-fated visit, 11-year-old Harper Gruzins turned in a truly shocking performance in front of 22,000 fans, and subsequently the entire world on the internet. The blog Deadspin described it as 'the worst national anthem rendition ever' and they weren't wrong.

TANNOY SONGS – EVERYWHERE
Probably the worst trend to develop in football stadia in recent years – and that includes endless post-match selfies – is the blasting out of 'feel-good' music as soon as a goal is scored. Not only is the music always awful, it completely drowns out the genuinely beautiful noise of a crowd going absolutely berserk.

MICHAEL JACKSON AND FULHAM
Michael Jackson was many things, but a football legend was not one of them. So when Fulham owner Mohamed Al-Fayed decided to erect a statue of his friend, who had once attended a game at Craven Cottage, outside the ground, some home fans were livid. But a couple of years later, the static Jacko was removed by new supremo Shahid Khan.

MUSICIANS WHO MIGHT HAVE BEEN FOOTBALLERS

Noel Gallagher is an impressive musician and song-writer, but a footballer he ain't. Which can't be said for this lot, who could all have been contenders before they found their true calling.

LUCIANO PAVAROTTI

Not only did he belt out football anthem 'Nessun Dorma' (OK, it might have existed before Italia 90), but the late, great Luciano also belied his gargantuan latter-day heftiness by having had a trial as a winger with his local team Modena FC when he was far younger. And lighter.

LOUIS TOMLINSON (ONE DIRECTION)

Weird one this, because one fifth of the world's most famous boy band *is* actually a footballer, but his appearance for Doncaster Rovers reserves in 2014 was more of a charity stunt than an attempt to force his way into the first team. His football pedigree includes running The Three Horseshoes pub team. He was also on the end of a shambolic challenge from Gabby Agbonlahor in a charity game at Celtic Park, for which the Aston Villa striker received 872 million death threats.

NICKY BYRNE (WESTLIFE)

The Westlife crooner really did almost make it to the highest level as he was one of the goalkeepers in Leeds United's 1997 FA Youth Cup-winning squad. He went on to try his luck at Scarborough and Cambridge United before playing for Cobh Ramblers in the League of Ireland. Byrne finally joined Westlife (not a football club), settling for a life where thousands of people screamed at him every time he performed instead of one where, er, thousands of people screamed at him every time he performed.

JULIO IGLESIAS (ASK YOUR PARENTS)

The Spanish singer was a promising Real Madrid youth goalkeeper in the 1960s until a bad car crash damaged his lower back and left him barely able to walk for two years.

MC HARVEY (ASK YOUR CHILDREN)

The So Solid Crew star was also a decent non-League footballer who might have made the grade had he not been busy doing whatever it was that So Solid Crew were doing. He turned out for (among others) AFC Wimbledon, Aldershot Town and Lewes.

ROD STEWART

The pop legend was a decent schoolboy footballer, who was spotted by Brentford while playing for Finchley Under-15s. According to his autobiography, he trekked over to west London for a trial with the club, tried his best in a five-a-side game, but never heard from them again. Rod went on to achieve extraordinary things, while the Bees... didn't.

DES O'CONNOR

For the purposes of this bit, we'll focus on Des as a singer on 36 albums rather than the chat-show or daytime TV presenter, OK? Good. 'During the war' Des moved to Northampton and turned out for The Cobblers' reserve team in the United Counties League. 'It was just after the war and the club were giving trials to just about any young lad who came along,' said club historian Frank Grand. Ouch.

MARK OWEN

Sealing a hat-trick for the boy bands, Owen was a promising young player who had trials at Manchester United, Rochdale and Huddersfield before a groin injury forced him out of football for good. He is a regular on the charity game scene, where he is always introduced as 'Take That's Mark Owen'.

GAVIN ROSSDALE

The Bush lead singer – and other half of Gwen Stefani, if you prefer – once had a trial with Chelsea. As you won't be surprised to learn, it didn't happen for him.

BAND XI

It was after the memorable Balotelli meets Gallagher extravaganza that we had a little attempt at a Band XI on Tuesday Team News. The results were simply punderful.

Team Name: Notorious PSG
Reserves: AC DC Milan
Stadium: Eminemirates
Training Ground: EtiHaddaway

Management Team
Backstreet Moyes
Simply Redknapp
Def Leopardew

First Team
The Beautiful Southall
Graeme Le Saux Solid Crew
Dizzie Pascal Chimbonda
Breen Day
Thuram Thuram (c)
Limp Busquets
Tchoyi Division
Guti & The Blowfish
Del Pierosmith
Musical Diouf
Red Hot Chilli Jeffers

Subs
Spink 182
Krul & The Gang
Guns & Moses
Dwight Bjork
Pirlo Jam
Kasabian Delph
ChumbaMuamba
Van Persie Sledge
Backstreet Boyce

Pop Tunes on Which Popular and Random Terrace Chants Have Been Based

What would football actually be like without music? Very, very quiet, as so many of the most common football chants – and some totally obscure ones – are based on chart hits. Like this lot, actually:

THE POPULAR POP CHANTS

'Go West' – Pet Shop Boys

First used by Arsenal fans in 1994, on account of their team regularly winning 1-0. Hence, 'One-nil to the Ar-se-nal.' The tune took off at grounds across the UK, with regular ditties ranging from 'You're pants and you know you are!' to the highly satisfying comeback chant of 'Two-nil and you messed it up!' Other words are available.

'Tom Hark' – The Piranhas

Most irritatingly used as 'goal music' but also more commonly in chants like 'Champions League, you're having a laugh' or indeed 'Top of the league, we're having a laugh'.

'Son of My Father' – Chicory Tip

An oldie but goodie, this 1970s hit became an anthem and is the tune for, among others, those Teddy Sheringham chants that used to start 'Oh Teddy, Teddy....'

'Seven Nation Army' – White Stripes

The modern-day chant for serenading pretty much every player with five syllables in their name. For example, 'Oh, Ro-bin van Per-sie!'

'Sloop John B' – The Beach Boys

The tune that is now used for at least half of all British football chants (based on no official statistics whatsoever). Fans of teams who think their players do whatever they please, for example scoring lots of goals, will sing 'We score when we want...', while Arsenal fans used to sing 'Adebayor, Adebayoooooor, give him the ball, and he will score'.

'Give It Up' – KC and the Sunshine Band
It all started when Crystal Palace fans started chanting 'Na-na-na-na-na-na-na-na-na-na Jobi McAnuff, McAnuff, Jobi McAnuff', and then others followed suit. For example, Newcastle fans chanted 'Na-na-na-na-na-na-na-na-na-na Demba Demba Ba' as did *loads* of others (but not all about Demba Ba).

THE COMPLETELY RANDOM POP CHANTS

'Sex on Fire' – Kings of Leon
Olympiakos manager Temuri Ketsbaia was roared on from the terrace as per the chorus of the famous rock hit:

Woah-oh-woah
Te-mu-ri Kets-bai-a!

'D.I.S.C.O.' – Ottawan
Sheffield Wednesday fans greeted Paolo Di Canio with this all-time classic:

He is D, he's delightful
He is I, he's incredible
He is C, he's from Celtic
He is A, he's amazing
He is N, he's a natural
He is I, he's Italian
He is O, O, O!
D I Canio
D I Canio!

'And I Will Always Love You' – Whitney Houston
Some inspired Crystal Palace fans once serenaded new French signing Alassane N'Diaye with Whitney's most famous chorus:

N'Diayeeeee, will always love you!

'Blame It on the Boogie' – The Jackson 5

Disgruntled Liverpool fans came up with this belter, poking fun at hapless defender Djimi Traore:

Don't blame it on the Biscan,
Don't blame it on the Hamann,
Don't blame it on the Finnan,
Blame it on Traore.
He just can't, he just can't, he just can't control his feet.

'Let's Talk About Sex' – Salt-n-Pepa

Arsenal fans had a bit of fun with the lyrics to the early 1990s hit with this ditty:

Let's talk about Cesc baby,
Let's talk about Fla-mi-ni
Let's talk about Theo Walcott, Freddie Ljungberg and Henry,
Let's talk about Cesc!

'Wonderwall' – Oasis

Manchester City and Oasis go hand in hand as we've seen earlier, and the fans were quick to adapt the band's megahit to Georgi Kinkladze and manager Alan Ball:

And all the runs that Kinky makes are winding
And all the goals that City score are blinding
There are many times that we would like to score again
But we don't know how
'Cos maybe, you're gonna be the one that saves me
And after all, you're my Alan Ball

'Too Shy' – Kajagoogoo

This 1980s hit had the lyrics 'Too shy-shy, hush, hush, ai-doo-aye' and Stoke fans must have been saving it up for years until they signed the right players. Suddenly, Tuncay Sanli, Robert Huth and Abdoulaye Faye were all in their starting XI:

Tun-cay, cay,
Huth, Huth, Abdoulaye!

MUSICAL INSTRUMENT XI

Now most football fans don't need any sort of musical accompaniment to come up with a little ditty. Occasionally you get a few drums and the odd trumpet thrown in, but here is a team XI inspired by the full range of the orchestra.

Team Name: Fiddlesbrough
Reserves: Panpipeanakos
Stadium: Ewoodwind Park
Training Ground: White Harp Lane

Management Team
Jose Tamborinio
Steve McClarenet
Horn O'Driscoll

First Team
Diggery Dudek (c)
Piccolo Toure
Sun JiHihat
Papa Tuba Diop
Claude Ukelele
Torsten Strings
GlockenTeale
Organ Gamst Pedersen
Adrian Flutu
AccorDion Dublin
DrumKitson

Subs
Violindegaard

Edwin Van Der Sitar
Pascal Chimbongo
Banjo Shelvey
VuvuZola

John Oboe Mikel
Sax Gradel
Benito Trombone
Saloman Kazoo

BY ROYAL APPOINTMENT

The royal family have had a lengthy link with football. They are always there at the cup final, Prince William is president of the Football Association and – legend would have it – a fan of Aston Villa. I know what you're thinking: the scarf he wears at Villa Park is always straight out of the box, but he's joined in his Villa love by David Cameron.

I went to Number 10 to see the PM a few years ago to talk about England's failed World Cup bid. He was also having a go at predicting the scores for that weekend in the Barclays Premier League. We set up in the Margaret Thatcher room and, in the end, Mr Cameron acquitted himself very well – better than one of his predecessors, Tony Blair, as you saw in the chapter on Football and Politics.

In the last few years I have also managed to bump into a couple of members of the House of Windsor. One went well… the other not so. Let's start with the good one. Her Majesty the Queen came to officially open the BBC's new studios in Salford back in 2012. I was asked to give her a little tour and I made sure to check what the correct protocol was when coming face to face with the reigning monarch. I knew 'chief' wouldn't go down well.

Apparently you don't extend your hand until she does, you call her 'Your Majesty' on greeting her and then 'ma'am' as in 'jam' from that point on. I was told I'd have three and a half minutes precisely with her and if I took any longer I would be harpooned in the neck by a ninja – I made that last bit up.

There was a gentle buzz around BBC North towers on the morning of her arrival – there were even a couple of burly security guards outside the bogs!

I went for the full suit but Mark Lawrenson opted for what Robbie Savage called his ice-cream seller's shirt. Didi Hamann was also in attendance and, while I was asking a question about Martin Jol's time at Hamburg, a voice announced: 'Her Majesty will be eight minutes early.'

Moments later there was a cheer outside followed by the patter of small royal feet approaching the studio.

Around the corner came the head of state wearing what I heard someone later describe as 'a nice little salmon number'. She was accompanied by BBC Director General Mark Thompson, who introduced me, and then off we went.

I introduced the ice-cream seller and Didi and explained what we used the studio for. I showed off our snazzy augmented reality graphics and explained that *World Football Focus* goes into millions of homes around the globe each week.

She asked a few questions about the appeal of football, Lawro cracked a couple of gags and I chucked in a stat about the fact that when Li Tie and Sun Jihai played for Everton and Manchester City respectively a few years ago the game between the two sides was watched by 300 million people in China alone. If you hear her palming off that in her next speech you'll know where it came from.

She had one last look at Lawro's shirt and left. No faux pas, no diplomatic incident and the word 'chief' never passed my lips. A number of people mentioned the difference in height between the two of us, with one comedian on Twitter claiming it was like watching Yoda meet Gandalf.

About six months after meeting Liz I also bumped into her husband. I was invited to St James's Palace to give a speech to some young people who had achieved the gold standard in their Duke of Edinburgh awards. The man was there to shake some hands.

It was during my speech that I was tapped on the shoulder by a palace official. 'I'm afraid the Duke is ready now,' he said. My joking suggestion that His Royal Highness should come in to hear the end of my address did not go down too well (Mistake 1).

The Duke strolled in and asked a few of the young people and leaders about their achievements, occasionally chatting to the proud parents. No one was saying anything and there was a really strange silence in a room of about 500 people. I can't bear an awkward silence.

As I waited in line to meet him, I remembered the one piece of advice/order I had been given on arrival: 'Whatever you do, don't ask him any questions.' That's a lot harder to do than you think.

'This is Dan Walker, he's a television presenter,' said the big man's mate.

'Hello there, how are you?' said the Duke.

'Don't ask any questions... Don't ask any questions' were the words wandering around my head...

'I'm fine, thank you, sir... How about you?' (Mistake 2)

The Duke ignored my question and ploughed on with the normal line of address: 'What is it you do?'

'I'm here to talk about my job to the young people, your honour' (Mistake 3 – he's not an 'honour', he's 'Your Royal Highness' or something). At least I hadn't asked a question!

'Of course, but what is it you do?' Prince Philip came back impatiently.

'I present a programme called *Football Focus* every Saturday.'

'Right,' he said, preparing to move on – but I couldn't help myself...

'If you ever fancy coming on, let me know!' (Mistake 4)
[Polite and dismissive laughter]

'We're one guest short this weekend if you can make it. Steve Bruce has pulled out!' I continued inexplicably. (Mistake 5)

At this point, I could feel the heat coming from the eyes of one of the Duke's aides. The parents in earshot were giggling and I heard someone muttering 'etiquette' in my direction as the royal party left the room. One of Prince Philip's advisors returned soon afterwards to tell me that 'one does not address the Duke like that'.

Thankfully I made it out with my head still attached at the neck and I haven't yet been summoned back to spend some time in the Tower.

THE PLAYERS WHO PULLED OUT LIKE BRUCEY

Steve Bruce left us one short at *Football Focus*, leading me to ask Prince Philip if he could fill in, which got me thinking about some of the most famous transfers that never happened because of a last-minute change of heart.

EMMANUEL PETIT

The Arsenal double-winning midfielder almost signed for Spurs, hours before he joined the Gunners in 1997. Petit arrived at White Hart Lane for a meeting with manager Gerry Francis and chairman Alan Sugar, and heard what they had to say before leaving – for Arsenal. He takes up the story: 'The day I arrived in England I first went to White Hart Lane. I had a meeting with Mr Sugar and they made me an offer. Two hours later they ordered me a black cab, it was pre-paid, and I went to see Arsene Wenger at his place. When I arrived he was with David Dein, and two hours later I'd given my word to Arsenal.'

WILLIAN

The Brazilian midfielder arrived in London for talks about joining Spurs (the jilted lover, again) in 2013. These talks took place and the player even had his medical, before skipping off to the open arms of Jose Mourinho and signing for Chelsea instead.

PETER ODEMWINGIE

A rare case of a player being jilted by a club as the West Brom winger decided he no longer played for the Baggies and headed down to London on transfer deadline day to sign for QPR – except Rangers didn't actually want him so he had to return to the Midlands with his tail between his legs. The full truth of this matter may never be known but the fiction is very entertaining.

STEVEN GERRARD

The Liverpool talisman very nearly became a Chelsea talisman in 2005 after Roman Abramovich parked his Russian tanks on Anfield's lush green pitch, metaphorically obviously, because he would have had to park them outside the ground. 'The reason the whole Chelsea thing came up was down to frustration that we were so far away from the title race,' said Gerrard. 'That's why this interest maybe turned my head slightly.' Fortunately for Liverpool, Gerrard's head was quickly turned back, and Chelsea missed out.

ALAN SHEARER

The legendary Geordie striker turned down Manchester United not once, but twice. Which takes some doing. Before he signed for Blackburn in 1992, he had an opportunity to move to Old Trafford but in his words: 'There was interest from Manchester United, but I was told I had to wait three or four weeks for them to get the money together. I felt if they really wanted me then they would come and get me immediately.' Then, in 1996, Alex Ferguson came calling again but Shearer chose to return to his roots in Newcastle. I have asked him many times... it was a move he never regretted.

There is a lot to like about beach-side radio studios. Sunglasses obligatory

PAUL GASCOIGNE

In 1988, Gazza could easily have been at Old Trafford rather than White Hart Lane, but, for once, it wasn't Spurs who were jilted. Alex Ferguson called missing out on Gascoigne the biggest regret of his career: 'We spoke to him the night before I went on holiday. He says, "Go and enjoy yourself, Mr Ferguson, I'll be signing for Manchester United." So I went on my holidays but Martin Edwards [then chairman] rang and said, "I've got some bad news – he signed for Tottenham. They bought a house for his mother and father in the North-east and that swung it." I think it was a bad mistake, and Paul admits it.'

CRISTIANO RONALDO

The Portuguese prince didn't exactly jilt the Gunners; Arsenal were actually denied by the fact Sporting Lisbon were asking too much money for the forward – at least according to the evaluation of Arsene Wenger. 'I had Ronaldo at the training ground,' says Wenger. 'But in the end it was a question of the amount of the transfer fee between the two clubs. Of course, he proved to be a bargain at £12.5 million, but the price that we discussed was in fact much lower.' Ouch.

DIEGO MARADONA

Read this sentence carefully. Second Division Sheffield United almost signed 17-year-old Diego Maradona in 1978. That's right, Maradona. Once again, it was only money that prevented the move from happening as the teams could not agree terms, although Blades manager Harry Haslam had been to Argentina and agreed a £200,000 fee for the teenager. Instead, Haslam signed Maradona's compatriot Alex Sabella for £160,000. He proved to be a little bit rubbish and United suffered back-to-back relegations.

The Worst Football Predictions Ever Made

The PM did a decent job with his football predictions on *Football Focus*, far better than some of these people, who really should have known better than putting their necks on the block by saying daft things.

Alan Ball

The Manchester City manager was in a positive mood when he signed Martin Phillips from Exeter in 1995 for £500,000. So positive was he that he declared Phillips would be the first British £10 million player. Three years later, he joined Portsmouth for £100,000.

Mike Ashley

The Newcastle United owner was feeling bullish when writing in the club programme at Christmas 2008, with the club two points above the relegation zone. 'Have a flutter on us climbing out of relegation trouble and into Europe,' he wrote. Words which were probably still echoing around his head when the Toon were relegated the following May.

Harry Kewell

The words didn't pass from Harry's lips, but his agent Bernie Mandic spoke for him after he opted to sign for Liverpool rather than Manchester United in 2003: 'Harry wanted to go to a club he felt were on the up. United have had a huge amount of success, but if you look at cycles, they are destined to go into a downturn, whether this year, next year or whenever.' Mandic and Kewell were right – it was whenever.

Malcolm Allison

The Manchester City assistant manager was feeling jubilant after the Maine Road club had won the league in 1968. Anticipating the challenge of the European Cup that lay ahead, Allison declared:

'We'll terrify the cowards of Europe.' Sadly, City lost to Fenerbahce in round one and didn't qualify for the competition again for 43 years – although they did win the Cup Winners' Cup in 1970, which is maybe what Allison meant.

Tommy Docherty

When the Doc saw Dwight Yorke play for Aston Villa against Manchester United in 1990, he was far from impressed and claimed: 'If Dwight Yorke makes a First Division footballer then my name is Mao Tse-tung.' Needless to say, Mao Tse-Tom is still eyeing up a significant slice of Pie De Humble.

Terry Venables

Previewing the 2009 Champions League final between Manchester United and Barcelona, El Tel was in no doubt as to whether he'd rather have Lionel Messi or Cristiano Ronaldo in his team: 'Messi is wonderful on the right but Ronaldo is terrific on the right, the left and through the middle as well. He also scores goals with his head, which Messi couldn't do even if they put a top hat on him.' Poor Terry probably couldn't look when Messi scored a fabulous headed effort to help Barca win the cup.

Pele

When the greatest footballer ever ever ever saw Ghana's Nii Lamptey playing in the 1989 Under-16 World Cup, he was in no doubt as to what he was witnessing. 'Lamptey is my natural successor,' said Pele, which was probably heaping *slightly* too much pressure on the African. Sadly, for personal reasons and many other factors, Lamptey's football career never took off in the way he, or Pele, would have hoped.

Cheyrou and Zidane not being like each other at all

Gerard Houllier

Another Liverpool manager to get carried away was the Frenchman, who signed Bruno Cheyrou and said: 'He will be a winner. He has great skill and some of the things he does remind me of Zidane.' Unfortunately, 31 Liverpool appearances in four years left Cheyrou looking like a rather pale reflection of Zizou... but he was French.

Rafa Benitez

In 2010, the Liverpool boss was so convinced his side would secure a Champions League place that he confidently announced to anyone who would listen: 'We will finish fourth.' Sadly for Rafa and Liverpool fans, they finished seventh, meaning they secured a spot in the Europa League – well, its third qualifying round anyway.

Ivan Golac

The Dundee United boss was so enthralled by the early performances of new Trinidadian signing Jerren Nixon in 1994 that he promptly declared, 'The boy will soon be worth twenty million.' A year later, Nixon was sold to FC Zurich for £200,000, which is actually only two zeros out.

FOOTBALLERS WHO WERE SO GOOD THAT THEY HAD THINGS NAMED AFTER THEM

Entering the Margaret Thatcher Room at Number 10 made me think about all the things that have been named after footballers – mostly its stands and the occasional few roads. But some of those road names are great and there's other stuff, too...

LEO WINE

In 2012, Argentine winery Bodega Valentin Bianchi created a range of reds and whites named after their country's most famous footballer. 'LEO' is said to be inspired by Messi's creative essence, which presumably means you can neck a glass then dribble round the busy pub twice.

LE ZLATAN

Parisian suburban restaurant Doddy's Cafe stock a ridiculously large burger named after Zlatan Ibrahimovic. The 600g of mince is served with onions, bacon and three types of cheese (well, this is France): Cheddar, Emmental and Bleu d'Auvergne. And with a price tag of 30 euros, it challenges both the wallet and the gut.

DROGBA BEER

If you're in the Ivory Coast for your summer holidays and order a Drogba at the bar, you won't get a 6ft 2in colossus, but you will get an ice-cold beer. Yes, the Chelsea striker is such an influential figure in his home nation that he even has a beer named after him. There's no higher praise.

BILLY WRIGHT TRAM

Never mind being the first player to win 100 international caps, the former England captain received the ultimate honour when the Midland Metro tram number seven was named after him. His daughter and granddaughter even turned up to the unveiling of the plaque.

STEVEN GERRARD TOWERS

'Hello, Mr Gerrard, this is Dubai calling. Is it OK if we name a one hundred and fifty million-pound apartment block after you, give you one million pounds and one of the apartments inside it?' It was an offer Steven Gerrard couldn't refuse – and he didn't.

BECKHAM CONDOMS

A similar conversation definitely did not take place between a Chinese condom manufacturer and David Beckham. But that didn't stop them naming their products after him, and sticking his face on the packets too.

CRUIJFF ASTEROID

Dutch star Johan Cruyff (or Cruijff in his native tongue) has a 9km wide asteroid named after him. The asteroid was discovered by Dutch astrologists and was formerly known by the rather less imaginative 14282.

TIM CAHILL EXPRESSWAY

And now for the roads… Sydney has a main road named the Cahill Expressway, after the former New South Wales premier John Joseph Cahill, the man who approved the building of the Sydney Opera House. But for 48 hours in 2013, the road was renamed the Tim Cahill Expressway, in order to inspire Australia to victory in their crucial World Cup qualifier against Iraq. To Cahill and everyone else's relief, they scraped home 1-0.

MESUT OZIL STREET

Next time you're on holiday in Turkey, you can take a trip to Devrek and stroll down Mesut Ozil Street. The road formerly known as 'Sand Houses Reedy Creek' was renamed in 2012 to honour the important work done by the German international in putting Devrek on the map. The midfielder goes there every year to visit his family.

ROYAL XI

After all this royal stuff there is only really one way to sign off this chapter... here is a fearsomely popular Royal XI.

Team Name: Luton Crown
Stadium: Rule Britannia Stadium

Management Team
Changing Of The Guardiola

First Team
Anne BoLindegaard
Duke & Duchess Of WayneBridge
McManus Horribilus (c)
Diamond Duberry
God Save Our Gary Breen
Lassana Tiara
Buckingham Palacios
Corgi Kinkladze
Ince Of Wales
George Weah-NotAmused
His Raul Highness

Subs
Zoff With His Head
Edwin Van Der Zara Phillips
Westminster Abidal
Baron Ramsey
Hatem King Arfa
Tropping The Koller

SPORT ON TV

'Time to come in now, Daniel' was one of my mother's most frequently used phrases. On this occasion I had been practising in the back garden for the best part of six hours. I was determined not to go back inside until I had rolled a football off the roof of the house and headed it between the edge of the kitchen window and the pole on the washing line – a gap of only 2ft.

As a boy this was how I spent my time. If I wasn't playing sport with friends I was practising in the back garden. My forward defensive backhand smash and left-footed free kicks had all been perfected just outside our back door. My dad's vegetable patch proved particularly useful. The runner bean rods provided an almost perfect defensive wall and at full height the curly kale could almost be a tennis net.

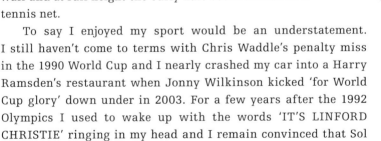

To say I enjoyed my sport would be an understatement. I still haven't come to terms with Chris Waddle's penalty miss in the 1990 World Cup and I nearly crashed my car into a Harry Ramsden's restaurant when Jonny Wilkinson kicked 'for World Cup glory' down under in 2003. For a few years after the 1992 Olympics I used to wake up with the words 'IT'S LINFORD CHRISTIE' ringing in my head and I remain convinced that Sol Campbell's goals against Argentina (1998) and Portugal (2004) should both have counted.

Most of my Saturdays were built around *Grandstand*. If you've never heard of *Grandstand*, it was the BBC's afternoon sports programme that started at lunchtime and went on until the football scores were in from the three o'clock kick-offs. There was none of this five-fifteen business. It included every sport imaginable, from the Winter Olympics to crown green bowls. *Football Focus* used to be a part of *Grandstand*.

I had a deep love for the programme, mainly because of the presenting powers of Des Lynam – who was like the perfect combination of Gary Lineker and Clare Balding, but with a moustache. At the age of 11 I wrote Lord Lynam a letter. It went along the lines of: 'Dear Des, I love your moustache. I like football. How do I get your job?'

To my surprise he wrote back within a week. On a single page of A4 'the chief', as I saw him, explained what he thought I should do to break into the world of sports presentation.

Des told me to work my way through school, finish my A levels and then go to university. Interestingly, he told me not to study 'media' but to read something like History or English, before doing a post-graduate course in journalism and then getting a job in local radio. When I did get a job in local radio at the age of 21 I wrote back to let him know I'd followed his advice to the letter. He never responded. I remain crushed by this. I potentially had a chance to thank him in 2005 when I won an award that he was handing out, but I had to miss the gong because it was the same night as the Champions League final in Istanbul. I have spoken to, and thanked him, since and he remains one of the finest humans ever to sit in front of a TV camera.

BBC World Cup studio, 2014. Seedorf did not approve of my choice of long-sleeved woollen number in 35-degree heat

Football Rituals

I may have spent far too much of my childhood obsessively trying to score a header into that 2ft space outside my house, but that's not a patch on some of the other rituals that have been used in football. Let's kick off with Basile Boli's girlfriend's lizard. Seriously...

THE LIZARD

Marseille defender Basile Boli prepared for the 1993 Champions League final in the same way you or I would any big match – by having his girlfriend sacrifice a lizard. Actually, he may not have known that much about it, but it did the trick as the French club won (although they were subsequently stripped of the title for financial irregularities). The incident confirmed the ancient Chinese proverb: 'Man who sacrifices lizard will eventually lose out in the Court of Arbitration for Sport.'

THE BACK ROW

Cristiano Ronaldo is a brilliant footballer but he's also a superstitious nut. When representing his country, Ronaldo always has to sit on the back row of the team bus, while he's the only player who's allowed to wear long sleeves on the pitch. If he was anywhere near average he'd never be allowed to get away with that nonsense.

THE WITCH DOCTORS

Before the 1992 African Cup of Nations final, the Ivory Coast sport's minister employed some Abidjan witch doctors to do their thing ahead of the match in Dakar between the 'Elephants' and Ghana. No one knows exactly what he did but it apparently worked as the Ivorians won on penalties. It's understood that no lizards were harmed during the process.

THE BLACK MAGIC

Qualifying for the 2006 World Cup was a great achievement for the Ecuador team, but they thought there was no way they'd go any further in the tournament without the help of black magic practitioner Tzamarenda Naychapi. He visited all 12 World Cup stadia to rid them of any evil spirits and bless them to be beneficial to the Ecuadorians – and it worked. Well, they made it through the group stage before David Beckham's free kick knocked them out in the last 16. Not even black magic can conquer Goldenballs.

THE VOODOO

When the Australian team faced a make-or-break match against Rhodesia in Mozambique to qualify for the 1970 World Cup, they dispensed with tactics and all that nonsense, instead employing the services of a local voodoo practitioner. Each goalpost had bones buried near it and the Socceroos ran out 3-1 winners. The story doesn't end there, though. The voodoo-ist wanted $1,000 for his troubles but the Aussies left without paying, and a barren period of international football followed, with seven successive World Cup qualification failures from 1978 to 2002. Then, an Australian documentary maker returned to Mozambique to try to lift the curse, which involved him being covered in the blood of a sacrificed chicken at the stadium. Lo and behold, the Aussies qualified for Germany in 2006 and reached the last 16. It might be tempting to think it was all down to the bloody-chickeny thing, but cynics have pointed to the fact that the Aussies had assembled a half-decent bunch of players for the first time in two generations.

THE WILLY WONKA

Voodoo and black magic are nothing compared to the antics of former Huddersfield Town player Malvin Kamara, who cannot step across that white line without having first watched *Willy Wonka and the Chocolate Factory*. 'I have to watch *Wonka* before every game,' he said. 'It gets me in the right mood. It's been my favourite film since I was little.' I have nothing more to say on this issue other than I love the fact he refers to the film simply as '*Wonka*'.

THE WEE
John Terry likes to listen to the same CD and park in the same spot before every Chelsea home game – so far, so standard footballer pre-match superstition. But, according to Frank Lampard, the man they call JT also likes to aim his wee in exactly the same spot of the same urinal before matches.

THE KISS
At the 1998 World Cup, France captain Laurent Blanc would plant a huge kiss on the bald forehead of goalkeeper Fabien Barthez just before the start of every game to make sure they won. And who could argue with that ritual as the French were crowned world champions.

THE STAR SIGNS
Staying with the French national team, when they ran out of kissy, kissy captains, unpopular coach Raymond Domenech devised other schemes, including a rumour that he picked players based on their star signs – which is allegedly why he once refused to select Scorpio Robert Pires.

Football's Greatest Injustices (Apart From England's Glorious Failures)

As I mentioned, I've still not come to terms with Chris Waddle's Italia 90 penalty robbing England of a World Cup, although it's just part of a long list of football injustices (not that the Germans will see it that way). These are some of the best – or worst. You know what I mean.

Chesterfield Cheated

The third-tier club were 2-1 ahead in the 1997 FA Cup semi-final against Premier League Middlesbrough when Jonathan Hewitt scored with a shot that bounced off the crossbar and in, to leave them with one foot in the final. Except the goal wasn't given. In the days before goal-line technology, the officials missed that the ball had crossed the line and the goal never stood. Although the Spireites eventually salvaged a 3-3 draw after extra time, their chance was gone and Boro advanced to the final after winning the replay. Gutted.

France Frazzled

France's Patrick Battiston was clean through on goal and about to score the goal that could have put France into the 1982 World Cup final when Germany's goalkeeper Harald Schumacher took him out in spectacular fashion, clattering into the player just outside the penalty area and getting absolutely nowhere near the ball. An obvious red card, right? Not even close. As Battiston lay unconscious, having lost two front teeth, broken his jaw and damaged his vertebrae, Schumacher was not even booked because Dutch ref Charles Gover did not deem the challenge to be a foul. To really rub salt into the gaping wound, the German then saved two spot-kicks in the subsequent penalty shoot-out to send Germany into the final. 'There is no compassion among professionals,' said Schumacher later. 'Tell him I'll pay for the crowns.' If there's a list of irritating Germans somewhere, he's on it.

Blanc Blanked

Staying with French World Cup injustice, Croatia's Slaven Bilic feigned injury in the 1998 semi-final after a penalty area tangle with France skipper Laurent Blanc. The captain was sent off and missed the final, what should have been the greatest night of his career. *Quel dommage.*

Platt Poleaxed

This could easily have been a list of England injustices only, but I've limited it to a couple. First up is the 1993 World Cup qualifier between England and Holland, when David Platt was clean through on goal and about to put England ahead and potentially into the USA finals. But then Ronald Koeman cynically dragged him down on the edge of the box. England cried penalty and a red card, but German referee Karl-Josef Assenmacher awarded a free kick and a yellow. Soon after, Holland took the lead with a free kick from the edge of the box scored by...? You know who. Robbed.

Spain's Pain

It seems hard to believe now, but there was a time when Spain were a hapless international team who followed one glorious failure with another. The 2002 World Cup was no exception, when they took on hosts South Korea in the quarter-finals in a game they won more than once, but not enough times for the liking of the Egyptian ref Gamal Al-Ghandour. Fernando Morientes twice scored goals that would have sent Spain through (one of them 'golden', remember those?) only for the officials to chalk them off. The Koreans eventually won on penalties and the world raged at FIFA. Anyone know the Spanish for *'plus ça change'*?

Malaga Mugged

In the 2012/13 Champions League quarter-finals, Borussia Dortmund were trailing Malaga 2-1 in stoppage time and on their way out of the competition. But two goals in the 91st and 93rd minutes saw them achieve a seemingly impossible turnaround –

especially when you consider both goals were clearly offside. In fact, the winning goal saw no fewer than four (F-O-U-R) Dortmund players in offside positions. Malaga boss Manuel Pellegrini, who had to fit in a round trip to Chile after the death of his father just before the tie, fumed: 'It was like there wasn't a referee on the pitch at the end, it was chaos in the closing stages, there were six or seven things which went unpunished in our area.'

Ireland's Ire

Extra time of a 2010 World Cup qualifying play-off game and Ireland were improbably holding France in Paris, their own proverbial back yard. Suddenly, Thierry Henry controlled a Florent Malouda free kick with his hand (twice) before prodding a simple pass to William Gallas, who scored to put France through. Cue bedlam, mayhem – the Irish were heartbroken, demanding the match be replayed and threatening to declare war on France (OK, that bit didn't actually happen). Henry did nothing to help the situation, saying: 'I will be honest, it was a handball. But I'm not the ref. I played it, the ref allowed it. That's a question you should ask him.' Cheated.

Diego the, er, Dastard

Thought I'd save the best until last. Everyone knows about it, but it doesn't get any easier to stomach even though it happened in 1986. England and Argentina were contesting a World Cup quarter-final with no score, when Diego Maradona, the best player in the world by some distance, contested an aerial challenge with Peter Shilton, put his hand in the air and slapped the ball past the England keeper and into the net. England protested, Maradona celebrated... and then scored the greatest individual goal in history. England were out. It was the 'hand of God' said Maradona afterwards. No it wasn't, Diego, it was a filthy bit of cheating, you dirty dog. That feels better, doesn't it?

THE MOST POPULAR ITEMS USED IN HOME FOOTBALL MATCHES

I made football matches come alive using anything I could at home. Here's my guide to the essentials every boy needs to replicate a football match at home.

PLANT POT

Not, under any circumstances, for plants, these are some of the finest makeshift goalposts known to man.

FRONT DOOR

Occasionally used to get in and out of a house, but always available as a small goal for those indoor sponge-ball games.

WASHING LINE

Remove any clothes and this makes the perfect crossbar for any temporary goal. Just remember, it is impossible to install a Goal Decision System on one.

WASHING-LINE POLE

If you're using the washing-line crossbar, you'd be a fool not to utilise this bad boy as your goalpost – don't make that mistake.

WHEELIE BINS

The more rubbish they contain, the sturdier they are – the deluxe version of the plant pot.

RUNNER BEAN RODS

As mentioned in the introduction to this chapter, if your old man has a vegetable patch, you won't get a better defensive wall to rehearse your set pieces with than these.

GARDEN SWING

Get the pesky swing out of the way. If it's one of those posh ones in a big frame you have a ready-made, but slightly irregular-sized, goal at your disposal.

FOOTBALL'S GREATEST EVER MOUSTACHES

In Honour of Lord Lynam

Despite remaining crushed by Des ignoring my letter, I've turned the other cheek to present the beautfiul game's most beautiful moustaches in honour of the great man. Let us together salute the lip hirsute!

Neville Southall

A no-nonsense, coiffured beauty.

Rudi Voller

If ever a look encapsulated German football of the 1980s and early 1990s, this was it. Exceptional.

David Seaman

Bright, bushy and brilliant.

Ruud Gullit

A moustache of two halves for a game of two halves.

Ian Rush

Could be mistaken for having been drawn on, but where would he be without it?

John Wark

Never a man to be curtailed by convention Wark had what was necessary to grow a lengthy monster and wore it with pride.

Vicente del Bosque

Distinguished, thick and wonderful – it's the tache that keeps on giving.

Rene Higuita

He could have been a long-lost South American cousin of Rudi Voller's. But he wasn't.

Brian Kilcline

Wild and terrifying, the Samson of taches gave Kilcline all his football strength.

Graeme Souness

If you felt that tickling your neck on the football pitch, you surrendered the ball immediately. Liverpool's dominance for much of the 1970s and 1980s was almost exclusively down to this prickly mo.

Charlie Paynter
(West Ham manager 1932–50)

An award-winning, mesmerising growth worthy of a place in the National Football Museum. Actually, that's where I found it.

TV Show XI

There is only really one subject matter that follows neatly from the subject of sport on TV. The world of television shows has always proved to be a rich harvest for the careful pun master...

Team Name: Lille Or No Lille
Reserves: Diff'rent Stokes
Stadium: A Place In The Sun Siro

Management Team
Some Mothers Do Avram
Klopp Of The Pops
Celebrity Bruce

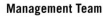

First Team

Only Kruls And Horses	Absolutely Fabregas (c)
Mysterious Cities Of Bould	Cabaye Got News For You
Teenage Mutant Ninja Skrtels	CSI Diame
Through The Keown	N'Gog Barry Avoid
Quedrue Do You Think You Are	Bodger & Baggio
Downton Xavi	

Subs

Nash In The Attic	Jerome & Away
Last Of The Summer Clyne	Zamorra The Explorer
Dan PetRescue	The Soldados
DrentheGhost	Call My Duff
Who Wants To Be A Willianaire	Super Nani
Late Dickov	Özil Gummage
Guppy The Vampire Slayer	One Foot In The Gravesen

THE CUP OF KNOWLEDGE

Alan Hansen hates stats. I am aware that he hates stats and keep telling him them for two reasons:

1. To annoy him, and
2. To see if I can ever find one that tickles his fancy.

During one breakfast at the 2014 World Cup I thought I'd cracked it: 'Al, did you know that IRAN are the only team in World Cup history whose letters appear in the names of all the other teams in their group?' (ARgeNtIna, BosNIA & HeRzegovina and NIgeRiA.)

As it came out of my mouth I could tell there was a backlash coming. Hansen took a lingering sip of his tea and pronounced through his regular smile: 'Dan, let me tell you, that's never been a stat. Where do you even get these from? I've no interest in any of that garbage.'

Anyone could play sweeper behind these two defensive rocks

But the thing is, football fans do love a random statistic. It's easy to go over the top but there is a passing interest in knowing that your team haven't won at Notts County since Queen Victoria was on the throne, or that Nikica Jelavic's last 15 goals have all been one-touch, or that Sunderland have never won a game on a Monday night in their history.

These are the sorts of things that fuel conversations and allow you to mentally prepare for a big sporting weekend. I do enjoy sending out a little social media nugget with a #statcave hashtag even though they normally illicit an understandable you-know-football-existed-before-the-Premier-League response from quite a few angry individuals.

In an attempt to celebrate the dazzling stat on my Friday night show on BBC Radio 5 Live, we came up with 'The Cup of Knowledge'. This mythical trophy was handed out to anyone who came up with a kernel of insight or a spectacular fact that blew the listeners away.

If I remember correctly, Danny Murphy and Pat Nevin received it regularly from the 'former players' stable and Jonathan Northcroft of the *Sunday Times* and Rory Smith of *The Times* led the way from Her Majesty's media.

So here are a few little beauties to allow you to bamboozle your friends. Use them sparingly and always try to casually drop them into conversation. If your compadres also have this book then you might be found out, but otherwise you are well on your way to a Cup of Knowledge. A final word of caution – none of these will ever impress Alan Hansen.

CUP OF KNOWLEDGE NUGGETS

Every single one of Hugo Sanchez's 38 goals for Real Madrid in the 1989/90 season was scored with his first touch.

When AC Milan was originally founded by two Englishmen in 1899, it was called Milan Cricket and Football Club.

Pele was the dirtiest player at the 1970 World Cup, committing 23 fouls (although he did play more games than most).

Sherlock Holmes author Arthur Conan Doyle played in goal for south coast amateurs Portsmouth AFC.

India qualified for the 1950 World Cup after all their opponents withdrew, but did not enter the tournament due to their football association failing to realise the importance of the event, and also because they weren't allowed to play barefoot.

Barnsley striker Ashley Ward put his side ahead at Sunderland in November 1998 after 33 minutes, missed a penalty moments later and was then sent off for stamping after 37 minutes, completing a rather unlikely five-minute hat-trick.

Fans of Dundee United have a unique claim to fame with which to taunt the mighty Barcelona as their side have a 100 per cent record against the Spanish giants, having played and beaten them four times out of four.

German goalkeeper Manuel Neuer has an acting credit to his name as he lent his voice to the character of Frank McCay for the German version of the Disney film *Monsters University*.

The first ever game played by a Brazilian national team was a 1914 fixture against Exeter City. Played at Rio's Laranjeiras stadium, the match saw a combined team from the host city and Sao Paulo take on the Englishmen, and win 2-0.

Cameroon midfielder Alex Song has a rather extraordinary number of siblings – 27, with 17 sisters and 10 brothers.

SCIENCE XI

Of course, stats and facts will only get you so far. If you really want people to think you are clever you need to conquer the world of science. This #TuesdayTeamNews offering won't get you all the way there but it's a start.

Team Name: LA GalaxoSmithKline

Manager
NeutRon Atkinson

First Team
Sonic Poom
Nemanja Physics
Herman Herydrogen
ChloroPhil Neville
The Big Bangura
Zola System
Dark Mata
Ji-sung Quark
E = Dempsey Squared (c)
Peter OdemStringy Theory
Hadron ColEidur Gudjohnsen

Subs
Darwin Van Der Sar
Sebastian LabCoates
Bruno Bunsen Burner
Remi OsMoses
Safety N'Goggles
Cameron Genome

THE BEAUTIFUL GAME

I consider 'Headers and Volleys' to be the king of football games. The rules are explained very clearly in the title and it also requires a degree of skill to succeed. I once tried to introduce this game to a group of Dutch kids on a Walker family camping holiday many moons ago.

Sadly, they had no interest in all of this and had also never heard of W.E.M.B.L.E.Y or 'Three and in'. They were far more interested in playing their game '*Vet Varken*', which I believe translates as 'Fat Pig' and involves nominating someone as the '*varken*' who then has to stay within a designated area while everyone whacks balls at them. Once they have been hit ten times, everyone shouts '*Vet varken!*' and then it's someone else's turn!

I know what you're thinking – 'How has this game not caught on in other parts of the world?' I am sure there must be variations on 'Fat Pig' outside of the quiet corner of rural Holland in the same way that 'It' in southern England was 'Tag' in the West Country, 'Tig' in the Midlands, 'Catchies' in Shetland and 'Tiggy Bob Down' if you were a bit odd and from Rotherham.

Despite my weird Dutch camping friends spurning the opportunity to play Headers and Volleys, it remains popular in all parts of the globe. I recall having a conversation about this with Yaya Toure during filming of a documentary about Barcelona before he made his move to Manchester City. Headers and Volleys was a firm favourite in the Toure household as he grew up and Yaya said they still played it in training.

We had a short stroll to the side of the training ground for a little insight into the 'Barca' version. Messi, Xavi and Iniesta were all standing about four feet away from an upturned stool.

Senor Guardiola was in charge and was watching and encouraging as they had to chip the ball into the legs of the stool, first with the right foot and then the left, before then collecting another ball the other side of the stool and volleying it past the mildly bored keeper. You couldn't shoot until you'd landed both balls in the stool. Once they'd found their range all three of them nailed the task with alarming regularity. Toure assured me it was a lot more difficult than it looked. I tried it in the back garden on my return home... We clearly have smaller stools in the UK!

We were in Barcelona for three days in total and one of those awkward foreign lift moments occurred. Arsenal had been beaten by Barca the night before in the Champions League and the following morning I was in a hotel lift on my way down with a fella who was reading a paper with a massive picture of Messi on it – he'd scored two goals in a 3-1 win. I said hello and, on discovering I was English, the bloke decided to embark on a conversation based entirely on the universal language of football.

'Messi, ohhhh!' he said, pointing to the front cover of his paper. Aware of my linguistic limitations, I responded in kind with, 'Messi, ohhh!' I thought that would be it but he took it up a notch... 'Messi, Messi,' he said smiling and pointing again.

I smiled back, lifted my shoulders into the universally acknowledged how-do-you-stop-him? position, and hit him with my own double 'Messi'.

He seemed to find this hilarious and kicked an invisible ball with his left foot before announcing the inevitable 'Messi, Messi, Messi'. Just when I thought this could go on for the rest of my life, the lift went 'ping' and the doors opened.

That trip remains one of the most bizarre and memorable of my career. We were there to film a documentary about the Barca brand of football and the way the club was run. It was one of those rare occasions when everything came together perfectly. During our time in Catalonia, Gerard Pique launched his autobiography, at which the whole squad made a surprise appearance, and Johan Cruyff was also awarded the honorary presidency.

To say they love Cruyff at Barcelona is a huge understatement. The Dutch master helped the club win La Liga for the first time in ages as a player and turned the whole place around as manager, winning 11 trophies in eight years.

As we entered the room where the unveiling was to take place, the Barca press officer said: 'I think you'll enjoy this.' He was right. When Cruyff came in he was followed by Eusebio, Sir Bobby Charlton and Ronald Koeman. Cameramen were climbing over each other to get the perfect shot. It was impressive to watch because no one jostles like a Spaniard – I'm sure they must practise at school.

At the height of the madness, Carles Puyol, Victor Valdes, Andres Iniesta and Xavi came in through another door while Pep Guardiola and Hristo Stoichkov strolled in via a third entrance. I half expected Pele and Diego Maradona to descend on a ceiling platform smothered in dry ice. Sadly, that bit didn't happen.

In the post-press conference melee, overlooking the Nou Camp pitch, I was involved in a conversation that still seems a little surreal. One of the club's press officers approached and said: 'Excuse me, Mr Walker, Eusebio, Stoichkov and Koeman can speak to you for your documentary.' They were all standing behind him.

Another media man tapped me on the shoulder. 'Sir Bobby Charlton and Johan Cruyff are waiting... but you have to do them right now.' We binned off the trio and went for the double. Spurning Koeman felt like a mild degree of payback for his goal against England in 1993, but the Dutchman was completely unaffected by it.

By the way... Cruyff had never heard of '*Vet Varken*'.

Famously Turned Down

I'm not sure that Koeman, Eusebio and Stoichkov were that bothered when I turned them down, although it did get me thinking about the players who were spurned by professional clubs at early stages of their career but went on to prove everyone wrong.

Kevin Keegan
The future England captain and manager was spurned by both Doncaster Rovers and Coventry in his teens, mainly due to his diminutive size. At the Sky Blues, managed by Jimmy Hill, Keegan was down to the final two at a trial but was overlooked. He finally got his break by playing with the Scunthorpe first-team squad in the club car park. Not sure if it was Headers and Volleys but he was offered an apprenticeship.

Kevin Phillips
The future European and Premier League Golden Boot winner was turned down by Southampton after serving an apprenticeship at The Dell. He failed to make it as a right-back so took a job stacking shelves at a Dixons warehouse while turning out for Baldock Town, before Watford came to his rescue.

David Platt
Many big stars have passed through the Old Trafford doors, only to be ushered straight out of them again. Robbie Savage and Peter Beardsley are two notable examples. But future England captain Platt was perhaps the biggest miss as manager Ron Atkinson's indecision cost the club. Platt was a YTS player at Old Trafford but, with strikers like Frank Stapleton, Norman Whiteside, Mark Hughes, Alan Brazil and the on-loan Garth Crooks, he 'wasn't even a regular in the reserves at that time'. He was sent out to Crewe on loan and when the Railwaymen tried to make Platt a permanent signing, he had a conversation with Big Ron. 'We're not sure whether to keep you,' Atkinson told Platt.

'I now know that he really meant it,' says Platt, 'that he didn't know what the next six months would bring. But I wanted to play so I left.'

Zlatan Ibrahimovic

When the young Swede was still a Malmo player he met with Arsene Wenger at Arsenal's training ground, as speculation gathered across Europe over who would clinch the striker's signature. Martin Keown remembers the day he turned up at training. His team-mates told a particularly feisty Keown that he was a new centre-half so Martin made sure he went in extra hard in that day's training session. There was no need to nobble comrades, though, as Wenger would only offer Ibrahimovic a trial period rather than commit to any long-term deal. This was not acceptable to the Malmo officials. Referring to this incident later in his career, Ibrahimovic famously said: 'Zlatan doesn't do auditions.'

Demba Ba

The Senegalese striker has a long list of clubs that initially turned him down before he went on to play for Newcastle and Chelsea. Among those teams were Watford, Barnsley, Swansea, Lyon and Auxerre, but Ba used that as motivation – he arrived at Newcastle saying: 'It helps that I have had to work hard to get where I am now at this great club. I have had setbacks. Everything happens in life for a reason, good and bad.'

Kenny Dalglish

Liverpool missed out on signing the talisman they eventually took from Celtic, when he joined the club for a week's trial as a 15-year-old in 1966. He actually played a B team game for the Reds against Southport but returned north to Glasgow. The following year, the Scot headed down to the bright lights of London for a trial with West Ham, but future England manager Ron Greenwood ruled that Dalglish was too slight to make it, and he once again headed back to Scotland where he signed for Celtic.

Joey Barton

The controversial midfielder was rejected by his local team Everton when he was 14. He went on to have trials with Nottingham Forest but was told he was too small to make it as a pro. Eventually, Manchester City picked up the teenager and Barton's professional – and occasionally troubled – career began.

Ruud Gullit

The Dutchman arrived at Bobby Robson's Ipswich already home to his compatriots Arnold Muhren and Frans Thijssen – as a 19-year-old back in 1980. Robson saw something in Gullit's attitude that he wasn't sure about so he passed on the opportunity to sign the future European Footballer of the Year. He wasn't alone, though, as Arsenal boss Terry Neill also rejected Gullit, balking at the £300,000 transfer fee reportedly being asked. 'Every manager has a skeleton in his cupboard – Gullit is certainly mine,' says a very honest Neill.

Gazza

Having once also considered John Barnes 'not good enough', Ipswich developed a reputation for refusing future greats. A 14-year-old Paul Gascoigne was similarly shown the Suffolk club's door after a trial. He was deemed too overweight to make it.

Andrei Shevchenko

In 1994, West Ham manager Harry Redknapp had the signing of the decade in his back pocket, but decided he didn't fancy him. He told the *Daily Mail*: 'I was at West Ham and Frank Lampard Sr and I were approached by these two villains who said they were doing some business in the Ukraine, and we were so scared of them we agreed to have a look at a couple of these kids. One of them we played against Barnet reserves and he scored the winner. They said they wanted a million quid for him, and Frank said it was too much – well, I'm blaming Frank – and we let him go. His name was Andrei Shevchenko.'

Eric Cantona

In 1991, Sheffield Wednesday manager Trevor Francis took the troubled French star on trial at Hillsborough but, due to poor weather, only saw Eric play one indoor game. Francis insisted that Cantona extend the trial so he could watch him play on grass, but Eric bid him au revoir and signed for Leeds, helping them win the league, while the boys from Hillsborough finished third.

THE PIONEERING PLAYERS WHO HAD FOOTBALLING PHRASES NAMED AFTER THEM

Whatever managers may say, some players are actually bigger than their clubs and even the game. So much so that a few of them, including the Barcelona honorary president, have been honoured by football terminology.

THE CRUYFF TURN

You've got to be pretty special to have a move named after you and Johan Cruyff definitely qualifies. The Dutch legend perfected the art of beating a defender with a trick he first used in the 1974 World Cup against Sweden's Jan Olsson. The move saw Cruyff drag the ball behind his planted foot, using the inside of his other foot, before turning away with the ball and leaving the defender looking like a confused idiot. It has been widely replicated ever since. I was once interviewing Cruyff and asked if he would be happy to replicate the move on camera with me. He looked me up and down in a very Dutch way and said: 'Don't be ridiculous. There is no way you can do it properly.' Crushed.

KOEMAN TERRITORY

During the late 1980s and 1990s, if a foul was given to the attacking side within 25 yards of the goal, the resulting free kick was always considered to be in 'Koeman territory', irrespective of whether he was actually playing or not. That's because Ronald Koeman made a habit of scoring from those positions, most famously in the 1992 European Cup final for Barcelona against Sampdoria at Wembley. He also – as we mentioned earlier – knocked England out of the World Cup in a 1993 qualifier (not that I'm bitter about it in the slightest).

THE PANENKA PENALTY

In 1976, the European Championship final went down to a penalty shoot-out between Czechoslovakia and West Germany. Antonin Panenka stepped up to take his spot-kick, knowing that a goal would win the tournament. Despite the scarcely conceivable pressure, he coolly hit a chipped shot that dropped straight into the middle of the goal as the German keeper Sepp Maier dived to his left. The penalty has been repeated often, with mixed success. Gary Lineker looked like he attempted it in a 1992 friendly against Brazil which would have given him a record-equalling 49th international goal, but his poor Panenka impression was easily pounced upon by the keeper.

THE MAKELELE ROLE

The defensive midfield position, made famous by Frenchman Claude Makelele, now bears his name. Makelele made his mark at Real Madrid by protecting the back four while his midfield mates made merry. He then perfected the role under Jose Mourinho at Chelsea. In simple terms, it's all about a lone midfielder, who sits in front of his defence, calmly breaking up opposition attacks before distributing the ball wisely. That, my friends, is the Makelele role.

RIGTIG JESPER OLSEN

In a rare case of an unflattering tribute, Danes call any hospital pass a *'rigtig Jesper Olsen'*, which translates as a 'real Jesper Olsen'. It is with reference to the former Manchester United midfielder's pass across his own defence, which allowed Spain to equalise against the Danes in the 1986 World Cup – a match the Spanish went on to win 5-1.

ROBINSONADE

In Austria and across central Europe, a diving stop or catch by a goalkeeper became known as a 'Robinsonade', after former Southampton goalkeeper Jack Robinson taught Austrians how to be a half-decent keeper. It's thought the phrase stopped being used after Paul Robinson's infamous air-kick for England against Croatia.

GARRINCHA TURN

The Brazilian's gift to football was less of a turn and more of a twist away from an opponent. As it has become increasingly common, it's not always associated with Garrincha any more, but he was the first to feign to go inside an opponent before using the outside of his boot to go outside and past his opposite number.

UNE PAPINADE

In France, a stunning acrobatic volley is known as *'Une Papinade'* after the great Jean-Pierre Papin, who made ridiculous volleyed goals his trademark during his career. They obviously haven't heard of Thronkers over there. We need to get this book translated into French. I am convinced it has the potential to be just as influential as *Asterix and Obelix*.

THE PUSKAS MOVE

The Hungarian legend gave us many things, including this fake pass classic in which he would roll his foot over the ball in one direction, before rolling the ball back towards him and heading off, or passing, in the opposite direction. It may sound simple but he was decades ahead of his time.

FIVE RETRO FOOTBALL GAMES

'Headers and Volleys' and '*Vet Varken*' were certainly classics of their time for outdoor football, but who doesn't love a football-based board game? Prepare for a trip down memory lane...

Blow Football

A physically demanding game that saw each opponent armed with a pea shooter and a goal to defend, with the idea being that the pea shooter would be used to blow the light, plastic ball into the opposition goal. Hours of lung-busting fun and a guaranteed red face and headache.

Kick-off

This game featured a set of cards and a board divided into little squares with one goal at each end. Each card featured an instruction as to what to do with the ball on the pitch – which direction to move it in and whether it was a throw-in, corner, shot, tackle, foul or penalty. The idea was to skilfully work out when to use the cards in order to win the game. If I'm being honest, I played it once and put it straight in the loft.

Wembley

A brilliant board game version of the FA Cup featuring all the Football League teams, including plenty that were last league teams when our dads were in short trousers. The idea was to try to guide one of your teams to the FA Cup final, while accumulating loads of cash as prize money. But in reality, it was fun enough to have all these cards with team names on that you could put into a hat and conduct your very own cup draw.

Subbuteo

A classic that still lives on in this digital age, as two sets of tiny, plastic footballers wearing even tinier replica kits went into battle controlled by two players who were allowed to flick, but never push, the plastic figures into the plastic ball to pass and score goals. I know it sounds like the dullest thing ever but one paragraph cannot do justice to the genius of the game.

Striker

The rival to Subbuteo saw much bigger plastic football figures that boasted proper kicking legs, playing a game of five-a-side on a much smaller pitch.

Unusual Football Club Mottos

Spending all that time at an institution like Barca was impressive. Their '*Mes que un club*' – 'More than a club' – motto tells you everything you need to know. But what of other football teams and their mottos? Well, they are not always straightforward.

GILLINGHAM
Domus clamantium – Home of the shouting men

BORUSSIA DORTMUND
Echte Liebe – True love

MARSEILLE
Droit au but – Straight to the goal

ROMA
La Roma Non Si Discute, Si Ama – Roma should not be discussed, but loved

KILMARNOCK
Confidemus – We trust

ELGIN CITY
Sic itur astra – Thus we reach the stars

FC ST PAULI
Non-established since 1910

KHONKAEN FC (THAILAND)
Beware the T-Rex

History XI

Football fans are very passionate about their history. Much of what defines supporters concerns great goals, incidents, moments of the past. The beautiful game is all about a celebration of what has come before, which is probably why the History XI went down so well.

Team Name: JFK Athens
Reserves: Declaration Of Independiente
Stadium: Ye Olde Trafford

Management Team
Offa's Dyche
The Third Rijkaard

First Team
Poomsday Book
Genghis Cannavaro
Breen Elizabeth The Hurst
Tugay Fawkes
NapoLeon Osman (c)
The Great Dyer Of London
Willian The Conquerer
Arteta The Hun
The Great Train Ribery
Bubonic Craig Bellamy
D-Day Drogba

Subs
Berlin Walcott
Moon Landon Donovan
TutanKanu
Huddlestonehenge
Thomas Blitzlsperger
Anne Brolin
The 7 Windass Of The World

THRONKERS

Back in 2003, one of my duties at Granada TV was commentary on the 'Goal of the Month' on *Soccer Night*. On one particularly dull night a colleague dared me to wedge in a made-up word. I accepted the challenge.

I selected a Mike Sheron volley for Blackpool that almost took the keeper's face off, he hit it so well. Here's my commentary: 'Here come Blackpool again, tidy cross in... Sheron... Oh, what a strike from Mike Sheron... WHAT A THRONKER!'

I was pleased with myself for having risen to the challenge, and the fellas in the office found it amusing. The executive producer – perhaps understandably – did not. 'Who is responsible for that?' he raged as he marched out of the TV gallery post-show.

'That might have been me, boss,' I offered with a nervous smile.

'Never again, Walker... NEVER! You can't just go around making up words. What on earth is a "thwonker" anyway?'

'It's a "thronker", boss,' I corrected, as the others in the office slumped further in their chairs to avoid making eye contact.

'I couldn't give a $%^$ whether it's a "thwonker", "thronker" or a "tonker"... you're a "plonker" and if you do it again... that's it.'

Despite its lukewarm original reception, I have conducted a low-level campaign for it to gain acceptance into the *Oxford English Dictionary* and Lady Susie of Dent from *Countdown*'s dictionary corner has given it her full support. Use it yourselves, people... They are watching.

The Rules of Thronk

There remains some confusion about what exactly constitutes a 'thronker', so much so that I've had to devise a tick list. There is obviously a loose definition akin to 'beauty', 'screamer' etc, but if you really want to get specific, pay close attention.

In order for a goal to be deemed a 'thronker' you must be able to answer 'yes' to at least four of these questions:

1 Does it threaten to lift the back of the net off the floor?

2 Does it come off the underside of the bar and then bounce high enough to hit the roof again?

3 Is it hit at full wellie? (none of this curler stuff)

4 Would it knock over a pig if it caught it full in the face?

5 Is it from at least 20 yards?

6 Did Tony Yeboah score it?

7 Does it make you go 'ooooh' when you see it for the first time?

8 Was it scored with the boot? (a header can never meet the requirements of a thronk)

9 Did it hit the side, back, roof of the net or crossbar (see rule 2) without bouncing first?

10 Was it scored in open play? (free kicks don't count – even the beauties)

11 Would it annihilate a pigeon?

If four of the conditions are met you have yourself a thronker. If seven are met, you are into double-thronker territory and if all 11 are relevant... you are into triple-thronker land (currently inhabited only by Tony Yeboah).

There is still much debate surrounding each one of the Rules of Thronk – so much so that a committee has been founded to clarify any contentious strikes. The committee is limited to four members and originally included me (of course), Tony Yeboah's mum, Jeremy Goss's milkman and Chris Kiwomya. After only two weeks into his role, Kiwomya resigned to spend more time with his family and Sir Clive Mendonca agreed to take up his position based solely on the fact that his name was only a syllable away from the real thing. The committee meets, via conference call, each time a great goal is scored to decide its status. Tony Yeboah's mum has the final say. The committee is clearly fictional but, as with most things in life, it's much more fun if you play along.

THE TOP TEN THRONKING FOOTBALLERS

TONY YEBOAH *TRIPLE*
Quite simply, the daddy of all thronkers.

STEVEN GERRARD *DOUBLE*
Capable of thronking from all angles – see that Champions League goal against Olympiakos in 2005.

DALIAN ATKINSON *DOUBLE*
There was a period in the 1990s when there was a campaign to make Dalian's middle name 'Thronker'.

Tony Yeboah. Enough said

MATT LE TISSIER
Once held his very own Thronker of the Season competition.

JORG 'THE HAMMER' ALBERTZ *DOUBLE*
This man went through a period of scoring nothing but thronkers.

ALAN SHEARER *DOUBLE*
Not a serial thronker but certainly responsible for busting the odd onion bag. Sorry.

CAMERON JEROME
You might be surprised to see him here but, my word, the lad can strike a football.

BOBBY CHARLTON *DOUBLE*
It could be argued that he invented thronkers but that would be daft because I did.

PIERRE VAN HOOIJDONK *DOUBLE*
A man who thronked regularly for club and country.

JOHN ARNE RIISE *DOUBLE*
The Norwegian has been known to annihilate the occasional pigeon in his career.

Real Football Words and Phrases That Sound Made-up

So 'thronker' isn't actually a real word (yet), but football already benefits from a dictionary's worth of ridiculous phrases that sound like they've been completely made up. Here's a selection from the land of 'football speak' which, when you stop and think about them, have almost no meaning at all.

Bouncebackability
It's not a word. End of discussion.

Six-pointer
Unless the rules have changed, the maximum reward for winning a league match is three points.

The Mixer
How, when and why did the attacking penalty area ever become known by this name? The 'box' will do just fine, thanks.

Back Stick
The things that hold the goal up are posts. That's it.

Onion Bag
It's a goal net. Onion bags are much smaller. If it was an onion bag it would be pointlessly big and impossible to move due to the fact it contains a couple of thousand onions.

Turned on a Sixpence
Nobody ever has, nobody ever will.

Wantaway
Only footballers with a desire to change clubs can be tagged with this. You never hear of wantaway doctors switching hospitals. It's football guff of the highest order.

Ace

No footballer has ever been described in such a way by anyone since the 1950s. The word briefly slipped back into use during the Campri ski-jacket craze of the 1980s but, despite that, tabloid newspapers will use it during the second sentence of a piece about any striker, e.g. the Macclesfield ace.

Plurals (Linekers, Shearers, Hansens)

If there's only one of them, don't pluralise. Nothing to do with me that rule... it belongs to the Lords of the English Language.

Cultured Left Foot

Culture is theatre, opera, arts or music – not a footballer's left foot.

Bite Your Arm Off

Football fans, managers and players are always being hypothetically linked with cannibalism. Which is strange.

Outfit

Club, side or team. There hasn't been an outfit since before the war. The first one.

Completely Made-up Football Phrases

And just for good measure, if those football phrases exist then why can't this lot? Here are ten that I'd like to see become part of footballing phraseology.

Rigor Mortis

The affliction suffered by footballers who score a goal against their former team and are not only unable to celebrate, but also instantly become completely motionless.

Simon Says Put Your Hands on Your Head

The reaction of a footballer who scores an offside goal, doesn't see the linesman's flag and continues to celebrate before realising nobody is celebrating with him.

Lazarus

The miraculous recovery made by a footballer who has been playing dead until he realises that the player who fouled him has been booked.

The Traffic Cop

The bizarre series of hand gestures performed by a substitute towards team-mates when he first enters the field of play.

Kenny From *South Park*

The stance adopted by a player who, substituted after a below-par performance, takes his place on the bench and adjusts the zip and hood of his tracksuit top accordingly.

Simon Says Put Your Fingers on Your Lips

The reaction of a footballer who scores a goal away from home in front of a particularly boisterous crowd.

You're Me Besht Mate You Are

As soon as a match goes to penalties this phenomenon sees team-mates spontaneously put their arms around each other in instant drunken-like friendship.

The Handcuffed Backward Shuffle

The ailment suffered by referees who make a contentious decision whereupon hands are immediately locked behind backs at the same time as backwards steps are taken to avoid protesting players.

Felix Baumgartner

A mysterious occurrence affecting goalkeepers who take on an aerial challenge with an outfield player for the ball. As soon as contact is made with an opponent, a rapid return to earth is made in the most dramatic fashion possible.

Playing a Blinder

The alternative version of this football staple is used when managers deny seeing anything vaguely controversial that one of their players might have done on the pitch.

THE TEN BEST PIECES OF FOOTBALL COMMENTARY NOT USING THE WORD THRONKER

While I can lay claim to the best piece of commentary using the word thronker, there are many others which have stood out over the years using more conventional vocabulary. For a variety of reasons, whether they're memorable, bizarre or just hilarious, these are my ten favourite pieces of thronker-less football commentary.

1. It's the commentary that would spawn dozens of newspaper headlines and thousands of tweets in the future. It's 1981 and the referee blows the final whistle to signal an ultimately meaningless 2-1 victory for Norway over England in a World Cup qualifier. Local commentator Bjorge Lillelien reacts in this calm, measured way:

> We are the best in the world! We are the best in the world! We have beaten England two-one in football! It is completely unbelievable! We have beaten England! England, birthplace of giants. Lord Nelson, Lord Beaverbrook, Sir Winston Churchill, Sir Anthony Eden, Clement Attlee, Henry Cooper, Lady Diana – we have beaten them all. We have beaten them all. Maggie Thatcher can you hear me? Maggie Thatcher, I have a message for you in the middle of the election campaign. I have a message for you: We have knocked England out of the football World Cup. Maggie Thatcher, as they say in your language in the boxing bars around Madison Square Garden in New York: Your boys took a hell of a beating! Your boys took a hell of a beating!

2. The 1996 Champions League qualifier between Danish side Brondby and Polish club Widzew Lodz was a dramatic tie with the Poles scoring a late, match-clinching away goal. It was all too much for commentator Tomasz Zimoch, who gave his best impression of a Sky Sports Fanzone rookie with this description of the closing stages:

Gooooool! Yes! Yes! Goal! Yeeeeeeeeeeeees! Who is the scorer? I don't know. Wojtala or Dembinski. The Danish fans are troubled. Widzew are losing three-two. Who is the scorer? It's not important but it's a goal.

It's the ninetieth minute – Mr Ahmed [the referee] let's finish it…. Another chance for Brondby but Szczesny catches the ball. What a nerve-wracking game. Daniel Bogusz is keeping his fingers crossed, sitting in the stands because he can't play today. Manager Tadeusz Gapinski straightens his smart hairstyle…

Ryszrad Czerwiec takes the ball on the right side, he is fouled… but maybe I exaggerate. It's a foul by Czerwiec.

Why doesn't the referee blow the whistle? On my watch there's ninety minutes. Goalkeeper Morgan Krogh plays the ball… there's no final whistle. Come back! Come back Poles and defend, Brondby are on the attack. Clear, clear the ball!

Oh, Dembinski has it. Go on, go on! He passed Colding, he's one on one. Dembinski versus the goalkeeper… Goooooo… No! Jesus Christ! What's going on? How could he waste such a great opportunity?

Mr Ahmed Cakar, let's finish it. Let's lose three-two but finish. Let's defend, Widzew. Three-two gives us a Champions League place. Michalski clears the ball. Kick it! As far as you can!

Clear the ball, we need so much experience now. Eggen is near the penalty area now. Czerwiec… no, it's Szarpak who heads it to the goalkeeper, he's allowed to catch it.

We're almost in the Champions League now. Nice pass by Szczesny, Dembinski on the right, on the left but he couldn't take it. Mr Referee, it's the ninety-second minute, there weren't any breaks, any injuries, why is the match still going on?

Widzew supporters are happy, the Danes are speechless. There are smart women wearing beautiful suits, smart men in white shirts and magnificent ties, but there's no happiness. They counted on great success, meanwhile Brondby are leading the match but are not going to make it to the Champions League.

Mr Referee, it's the ninety-third minute… Widzew in a

counter-attack, Citko passes to Szarpak but Morgan Krogh grabs the ball. Mister, why don't you blow the whistle? Mister Turk, you should finish this gaaaame... Szczesny catches the ball fourteen metres from the goal...The Turk! Finish this game now!

Widzew clears the ball, Szarpak plays it, but it's irrelevant. Brondby look resigned. Yes, don't let him play, take the ball!

Another chance for Brondby, Widzew are defending really deep... Oh my God! What's going on? Another opportunity on the left wing. The chance is gone. Daugaard heads the ball and a Widzew player probably handles the ball.

And that's it! The final score three-two. It's defeat but we are in the Champions League!

3. Former Newcastle footballer Ray Hudson (29 appearances, they all count) now plies his trade as an English language commentator for an American 'soccer' channel, beIN Sports. And he uses the English language in a unique way. Here's a sample description of a Lionel Messi goal for Argentina against Venezuela:

Like a Jedi knight, thou art better than that – a Templar Knight, this is a flash of pure inspiration and let me tip my hat to the genesis of this goal – Ibarra. Lionel only absolutely lights it up here, he lifts off it, flamethrowers it past poor Renny Vega. It's just as well Renny didn't get a hand to that because it would have taken it off his wrist. Superlative football, it was an out of this world, Bernini-sculpture of a finish. Majestical Argentina and merciless – like Kathy Bates with a sledgehammer in that movie. Remember that, *Misery*? That's what Messi was like, he pulled a sledgehammer out.

4. Juan Manuel 'Bambino' Pons is an Argentine commentator for Fox Sports who doesn't settle for just talking into the mic. Instead, he celebrates a goal by singing and he has signature tunes for many Premier League players. When Paul Scholes once put Manchester United ahead of Liverpool, he sang the following over the opening chords of 'Eye of the Tiger':

Gol.
Gol de Scholes,
Gol de Schoooooles.

He also sings a cover version of Abba's 'Fernando' for a Torres goal while Thierry Henry used to get his name chanted to the tune of operatic aria 'O Sole Mio' for no apparent reason.

5. 'Ding-Dong' Dave Higson is the only official club commentator on this list but he was no ordinary official club commentator. Higson, who called all Bolton matches, would greet almost any goal with his catchphrase 'What a ding-dong do!' Once, when a late John McGinlay goal sparked a pitch invasion, high-pitched Higson commented in his Lancastrian tones: 'And the fans are on the pitch. They think it's all over – just like the World Cup.' Best of all was Higson's reaction to an injury-time winner for Port Vale against his beloved Wanderers:

Oh dear me. A well-taken goal there... but one thing I must ask, we're not quite sure what time this referee is playing to. It's now four minutes to five on my watch here. One wonders just how much injury time he's played. And there goes the final whistle. Dear me, I think the referee has a white shirt on. There's no doubt about that. Today's match referee... one wonders whether he's come on the Port Vale team bus.

6. The 1998 World Cup quarter-final between Argentina and Holland was all square in the 89th minute when Dennis Bergkamp received a long ball on the edge of the penalty area from Frank de Boer. The Dutchman brought it down first time with a sublime touch, before flicking it past Roberto Ayala and then steering the ball into the top corner of the net with the outside of his right boot to send Holland into the last four. And this is how Dutch radio commentator Jack van Gelder described those moments:

Dennis Bergkamp, Dennis Bergkamp, Dennis Bergkamp, Dennis Bergkamp... DENNIS BERGKAMP. Oooooooooh!

7. The 1966 World Cup final is famous for Kenneth Wolstenholme's 'They think it's all over' line but arguably his greatest words were saved for the moment when Bobby Moore was about to lift the Jules Rimet trophy:

It's only twelve inches high... solid gold, and it means England are the world champions.

8. The last 30 seconds of the 1988/89 league season saw Arsenal needing one more goal to beat Liverpool, who were top, 2-0 and win by enough goals to claim the title themselves. The legendary Brian Moore called it like this and 'It's up for grabs now' became an iconic commentary moment:

Arsenal come streaming forward now in surely what will be their last attack. A good ball by Dixon finding Smith... to Thomas charging through the midfield... Thomas! It's up for grabs now! Thomas! Right at the end! An unbelievable climax to the league season.

9. Another incredible climax involving Arsenal was described by BBC Radio's Peter Jones. The 1979 FA Cup final had seen the Gunners lead 2-0 before two late Manchester United goals seemed set to take the game into extra time. Then this happened:

Here comes Brady though for Arsenal. They still perhaps want to finish it off before extra time. The ball floats high across the area, the shot comes in, it's there! Alan Sunderland! It's three-two for Arsenal and I do not believe it. I swear I do not believe it.

10. For all the flowery language and emotion used by commentators, sometimes simple is best. Here's how David Coleman described Allan Clarke's match-winning goal for Leeds in the 1972 FA Cup final against Arsenal:

Clarke. One-nil.

SOCIAL MEDIA XI

The 'thronker' is a very powerful tool in the world of social media so it seems only right that we use the end of this chapter to combine the world of football with social media via the power of the pun.

Team Name: InstaGrampus 8
Reserves: Poke City
Stadium: Stadium Of Like
Training Ground: Filbert Tweet

Management Team
Martin Troll
Trendin' Rodgers
Ian LOLoway
Laudrupbox

First Team

Carlo Nashtag	Jonjo Selfie
MSN Boyce	Mohamed DM Me
HashTaggart	LinkedInamoto
Yolo Toure	Snap Chapuisat
Bebo Balde	Wiki Lambert
PhotoBommel (c)	

Subs
Steve Blogrizovic

Sun JiHispace	Pinterescu
SoundCloudio Pizarro	Tweeter Crouch

WHEN LEGENDS MEET LEGENDS

Famous footballers can often have an odd effect on members of the general public. I remember watching (and helping, by the way) a middle-aged lady when she clapped eyes on Alan Hansen coming out of a lift. Seeing the Scotsman's forehead scar up close was all too much for her.

I interviewed David Beckham at the offices of the Mayor of London during the 2012 Olympics and as we exited the room there was a clutch of individuals waiting for a sight of an immaculately groomed Mr Beckham. One of the gathered throng – a lady in her forties I would estimate – burst into tears at the sight of his excellently coiffed quiff and another – a very well-to-do businessman – couldn't stop laughing when David asked him if he was OK. The bloke was rendered incapable of speech as David tried again. 'It'll be fun tonight,' he said, referring to the opening ceremony, but again he was met with slightly confused giggles and an ever-reddening face.

I am sure the fella tells his friends and family how he and Dave 'hung out at the mayor's place' but the truth was a little different.

Footballers always seem cool. Most of the time they are well-dressed, arrive fashionably late, are followed around by autograph-hungry youths and are almost always the most famous person in a room.

I was once asked to host a big corporate get-together for ten sportsmen and women who were all sponsored by Nike. There were some big-hitters in the building: Didier Drogba, Ashley Cole,

Cesc Fabregas and Theo Walcott from the world of football were joined by Mark Cavendish, Paula Radcliffe, Allyson Felix and a snowboarder from Finland called Peetu Piiroinen, who wore a massive hat for the entire event.

Between them they had a serious number of gongs and achievements but the man with the biggest mantelpiece of them all was introduced last. Carl Lewis has endless Olympic and World Championship gold medals to his name and the International Olympic Committee voted him 'Athlete of the Century' – the sort of title that calls for an instant reordering of business cards.

The crowd were very excited to see the famous faces and the footballers took it all in their comfortable strides, raising hands aloft to acknowledge the fact that they were just as cool as their adoring public thought they were.

It was fascinating to see Drogba's body language change when he met Lewis. He started giggling and looked a little bit like a four-year-old who'd just been given a life-size Buzz Lightyear for his bedroom. Lewis had been one of his heroes when he was growing up and during the pre-event chat he was talking me through his favourite memories. I can't recall all of what he said because I got distracted by the arrival of some fruit kebabs.

Each athlete had been asked to bring a memento from their career and it was interesting to watch the footballers strangely drawn to Fabregas' World Cup final boots, which seemed to have a similar power to the Stone of Orthanc from *Lord of the Rings*. Drogba gave them a tentative jab and Cole stroked them knowingly. For some reason there was almost no interest in my Keegan Patricks.

David went conventional crossed-legs; I opted for the 'tuck'

Football's Most Famous Tears

As hard as it might be to believe, there have been a few tears at football matches that have had nothing to do with David Beckham's quiff. Hankies at the ready – here's a selection of football's teariest moments.

Rod Stewart

Not all tears are shed on the pitch; a fair few roll down cheeks in the stands, especially Rod Stewart's at Parkhead in 2012. Rod cried great big salty tears of joy after Celtic beat Barcelona in a Champions League group match. Just as well for Rod that the Bhoys never made it past the last 16.

West Ham Fan

Nobody wants to see a child reduced to tears on national television – unless they're a contestant on *Britain's Got Talent*, of course. One young West Ham fan had travelled all the way to Nottingham to see his side get stuffed 5-0 by Forest in a 2014 FA Cup tie, and was captured by cameras bawling his eyes out, which prompted some to slightly harshly condemn Hammers boss Sam Allardyce for child abuse.

John Terry

After snatching defeat from the jaws of victory by missing his penalty in the 2008 Champions League final, JT sobbed his heart out in the Moscow rain and then on Avram Grant's shoulder, with complete disregard for his manager's brand-new cup final suit. 'We couldn't stop him crying,' said Ricardo Carvalho. We know.

Paul Gascoigne

Arguably the most famous tears in football history; certainly the best known since British on-pitch blubbing records began. He cried briefly when he picked up the 1990 World Cup semi-final yellow card that meant he would miss the final, and then sobbed uncontrollably after the match when it turned out he wasn't the only England player missing the final.

Pele

Gazza's World Cup tears were certainly not the first; Pele beat him to it by a good 32 years when he lost the plot after helping his country win its first Jules Rimet trophy. The 17-year-old future Galactico used the shoulder of his team-mate Didi to hide his emotion but everyone knew he wasn't just having a cheeky cuddle.

Eusebio

The Portuguese prince also left the pitch in tears in 1966, but these were bitter blubs of defeat, after his country had lost their semi-final against England. If he'd been able to know the result of knockout matches between the two countries in the 2000s it may have possibly tempered his quivering lip.

Bayern Munich

'That night in Barcelona,' as someone once said. Spare a thought for the crestfallen Bayern Munich players who had one hand, and four fingers, on the trophy as they led 1-0 in stoppage time. But, as Clive Tyldesley famously said... Manchester United always score. The emotion of it all reduced massive human Carsten Jancker to sobs and team-mate Samuel Kuffour into ground-beating disbelief.

David Seaman

A serial blubber? You bet. 'Safe hands' was led from the Wembley pitch in tears by the late, great David Rocastle after Arsenal lost to Spurs in the 1991 FA Cup semi-final. Eleven years later, he was at it again after Ronaldinho caught him napping to put Brazil into the World Cup semi-final at the expense of England.

Cristiano Ronaldo

The winkmeister is another double blubber, who shot to teary fame on the international stage after Portugal lost the Euro 2004 final to Greece. A year later, he was in need of some Portuguese tissues again when Manchester United lost the FA Cup final on penalties to Arsenal.

Mario Balotelli

Everyone's favourite mad striker didn't bother to wait for a heart-breaking defeat in a huge match to make his crying debut. Instead,

Mario broke down in tears on the AC Milan bench when he was substituted during the 3-1 defeat to Napoli in a 2014 Serie A match.

Roberto Baggio
'The Divine Ponytail' cried tears of joy when Italy beat Bulgaria to reach the 1994 World Cup final. But he was soon shedding bitter tears of despair when he became the third Italian to miss in the penalty shoot-out that gave Brazil victory in the final. That, stats fans, is the first time a World Cup has been won in that manner. You are allowed to dazzle your pals with that one.

Diego Maradona
The sleight-of-hand merchant, responsible for so many English tears in 1986, was spotted crying big wet ones after Argentina were defeated in the 1990 World Cup final by Germany. Poor old Diego.

Jong Tae-se
Perhaps the greatest World Cup tears of the lot, this North Korean player suffered a complete emotional breakdown during the 2010 tournament, sobbing uncontrollably. But he hadn't missed a penalty, nor had his country been knocked out. Instead, this was simply Jong's intensely patriotic reaction to the national anthem before his country's opening match against Brazil. He started a trend, as anthem-blubbing caught on in Brazil four years later, with home hero Neymar and Ivory Coast's Serey Die winning the Golden Bawl.

THE SCARIEST SCARS IN FOOTBALL

Having been up close and personal with it on more than one occasion, Alan Hansen's scar is mightily impressive and it was no surprise that middle-aged lady required help. He's not the only footballer who has had a mark left on him.

Franck Ribery

The French wing wizard had one hundred stitches on his face after being seriously injured in a car crash when he was a child.

Carlos Tevez

The Argentine striker was accidentally scalded with boiling water as a child and suffered bad burns, but he has always refused many offers of plastic surgery preferring to stay 'natural'.

Joleon Lescott

The defender was hit by a car when he was a child and picked up a permanent souvenir for his troubles.

Gael Clichy

The full-back's ring finger is scarred after it had to be sewn back on when it was caught on a fence.

Salomon Kalou

The striker has stud marks all over his feet as he played for two years in the Ivory Coast without boots. Judging by the dents, his opponents were definitely booted.

'Hanging Out With Beckham'... how footballers and managers don't tend to see things the way everyone else does

Our friend at the mayor's office who could only giggle and go red in the face while David Beckham talked to him, and then probably dined out on stories of hanging out with the footballer, is not alone when it comes to having his own version of events. Oh no.

WE SEE: Manchester United midfielder Marouane Fellaini's forearm smash into the face of Manchester City's Pablo Zabaleta in a 2014 Premier League derby.

DAVID MOYES SEES: 'My first feeling is it wasn't even a free kick... My feeling at the time was that he's just back[ed] into the player and there's nothing in it.'

WE SEE: Diego Maradona jumping in the air with Peter Shilton and guiding the ball with his hand into the goal in the 1986 World Cup quarter-final.

MARADONA SEES: '[The goal was scored] a little with the head of Maradona, and a little with the hand of God.'

WE SEE: Liverpool's Luis Garcia scores a highly disputed goal during the 2005 Champions League semi-final second leg against Chelsea. TV replays fail to show conclusively whether the ball crossed the line.

RAFA BENITEZ SEES: 'After the game, Sheila [club secretary], who was sitting right in line in the main stand, said to me that the ball had crossed the line. She is a very honest person and that was good enough for me... it was a goal.'

WE SEE: Arsenal's Patrick Vieira is fined £45,000 and banned for six matches for spitting at West Ham's Neil Ruddock after being sent off.

ARSENE WENGER SEES: 'Patrick is not a dirty player. His attitude is right and I don't think this will affect his aggression on the field.'

WE SEE: Manchester United's Roy Keane reveals in his autobiography that his horrific challenge on Manchester City's Alf-Inge Haaland was premeditated.

ALEX FERGUSON SEES: 'I don't think Roy has anything to worry about. I don't think there's a case to answer.'

WE SEE: Manchester City's Ben Thatcher knocks Portsmouth's Pedro Mendes unconscious with a brutal tackle.

STUART PEARCE SEES [BEFORE BEING SHOWN A REPLAY]: 'I want the players to play at a high tempo near the ball and it looks like the tackle was a bit mistimed.'

WE SEE: Arsenal's 49-game unbeaten run ended fairly and squarely at Old Trafford as they lose 2-0 to Manchester United.

ARSENE WENGER SEES: '[Referee Mike] Riley decided the game, like we know he can do at Old Trafford. We were robbed.'

WE SEE: Thierry Henry handle the ball to set up France's play-off winner against Ireland which means they qualify for the 2010 World Cup.

GERARD HOULLIER SEES: 'He didn't cheat. It was instinctive.'

WE SEE: Zinedine Zidane head-butts Marco Materazzi in the chest towards the end of the 2006 World Cup final and is sent off in disgrace.

FRENCH PRESIDENT JACQUES CHIRAC SEES: 'I don't know what happened, why Zidane was punished. But I would like to express all the respect that I have for a man who represents at the same time all the most beautiful values of sport, the greatest human qualities one can imagine, and who has honoured French sport and, simply, France.'

THE FOOTBALL HEADWEAR STYLE GUIDE

That permanently hatted Finnish snowboarder got me thinking about the use of headwear in football. And it got me thinking so much that I came up with this collection of nine football headwear essentials.

Petr Cech's Protective Helmet

After his shocking injury at Reading, the Chelsea goalkeeper became synonymous with the rugby-style protective helm. It became so popular with Chelsea fans that they even created a song for it:

> *Petr Cech has got his hat on,*
> *Hip-hip-hip-hip-hooray,*
> *Petr Cech has got his hat on,*
> *'Cos without it he can't play*

Chris Kirkland's Baseball Cap

Not as popular as it used to be in the 1980s, but the goalie's baseball cap still makes the odd unscheduled appearance, with Wigan's Kirkland the last top-flight keeper to wear one, in 2009 against West Ham.

Tony Pulis's Baseball Cap

The Welshman loves a cap and would never be seen on the touchline without one, going against the suit, tie and overcoat look of so many of his Premier League counterparts. He's not the only manager to sport the cap, as Leyton Orient's Russell Slade also wears one to cover his shiny bald pate – only removing it when serenaded about said bald pate by O's fans.

Gazza's Face Mask

Not strictly top-of-the-head style, but the *Phantom of the Opera* look became de rigueur after Gazza wore one during his recovery from a facial injury. John Terry, Paolo Maldini and even Gary Mabbutt were among the in-crowd who went on to wear one.

Jonas Gutierrez's Spiderman Mask

A highly sought-after and unique piece, this mask is only aired during the winger's goal celebrations in which he whips it out in the manner of a magician and runs around, shooting imaginary webs at fans. A niche accessory.

Wayne Rooney's Syrup (OK, it's a hair transplant)

Rooney's drastic action of undergoing surgery to grow some hair back on to his thinning bonce has yet to have the trendsetting impact he might have hoped for, but it's early days. The most likely player to follow suit will be Rooney himself, as there is no lifetime guarantee.

Efe Sodje's Bandana

The lower-league journeyman and Nigeria 2002 World Cup star has never played without a bandana on his head. And that's because back in 1994 his mother told him to wear one while he played to ward off evil spirits.

Terry Butcher's Blood-soaked Bandage

The original look of the hard man, the bloody bandage was first spotted on the England defender during a World Cup qualifying goalless draw against Sweden in 1989 which ensured England reached Italia 90. Eight years later, Paul Ince repeated the look in another gutsy 0-0 in Italy to book England's place at France 98.

Edgar Davids' Glaucoma Goggles

Perfect for those sunny afternoons, the Davids goggles also work for evening matches as they repel the intensely dazzling gaze of the floodlights.

Footballers' Heroes

So the young Drogba was obsessed by Carl Lewis, but who were the footballing idols of other players? This way please...

Marouane Fellaini

The big-haired Belgian dreamed about playing like someone with far less on top when he was a mere urchin. 'There are a lot of great players – Ronaldo, Messi... but I loved Zidane,' says Fellaini. 'When he played he made it seem like he was playing in the garden.'

Mario Balotelli

Who does a predatory striker in the making look up to in his formative years? Why, another predatory striker, of course: 'When I was a kid my idol was Ronaldo,' says Mario. 'He was a fantastic player who made me fall in love with the game.'

Alex Buttner

If you're a Dutch kid growing up in the 1990s and noughties, there's only one legend you wanted to emulate. Dennis Bergkamp, right? Wrong. 'When I was young, my hero was Johan Cruyff,' says Buttner. 'I never saw him play live as I was too young, but I watched him on DVDs that my dad, and pretty much everyone in Holland, owned. He played for Ajax, like I did, and his confidence inspired me.'

Aaron Ramsey

Ah, the football legends who inspire the wannabe kids. Their names roll off the tongue: Cruyff, Zidane, Kavanagh... eh? 'Graham Kavanagh. He was the Cardiff captain and played in my position so that's who I looked up to and wanted to aspire to be like,' says Ramsey. Perhaps the Ramseys didn't have a telly?

Samir Nasri

Samir Nasri is not afraid of a little controversy, so his idol is not so surprising: 'Maradona – even though I was born the year after he won the World Cup,' he says. 'My father loved him, and I had video tapes of him in action. I watched his games from 1986 over and over again. I absolutely loved him. For me, he was the best. He was one of my main inspirations to become a footballer.'

Xavi
If you're a very young Barca fan in the 1980s, there's only one man you're going to look up to. 'Initially [my idol was] Bernd Schuster,' says Xavi, 'but when I began training with Barcelona it was Josep Guardiola, who became my coach.'

Carles Puyol
Another Barca legend has a less obvious football hero. Puyol is infatuated by AC Milan stalwart Paolo Maldini. So much so that when the defender retired, Puyol wrote him what must be one of the most gushing letters of all time: 'You began your playing career when I was a child and I never stopped admiring you,' he wrote. 'People say that when you grow up, you lose your idols. But not me. I continue to admire you more and more.' Pass the bucket, please.

Stan Collymore
The Villa fan only had eyes for his claret-and-blue heroes in the early 1980s. Asked who his childhood hero was, Stan the Man said: 'Gary Shaw! He was great on the ball, could twist and turn, weighed in with goals and he was a big inspiration for me to try and go on and be a professional footballer.'

Phil Jones
George Best? Pele? Maradona? Nope, nobody. Jones had no childhood football crush whatsoever. 'I tried to model my game on good centre-backs in the Premier League, really,' says Jones. 'There wasn't one specific player that really influenced me. I'm often asked that question but I never idolised one individual.' Not even Graham Kavanagh?

Steven Gerrard
Stevie G must love watching *Match of the Day* every week, even when Liverpool lose. And that's because he grew up idolising Gary Lineker. 'I had him on my bedroom wall,' admits Gerrard. 'He was someone who I looked up to growing up.' Well, you would have had to if he was on your wall.

FILM XI

Perhaps the most popular #TuesdayTeamNews of all time was the Film XI which was the number one trend in the world for about three hours a few years ago – absolute madness. While we are talking about legends it seems only right that the most popular pun subject takes centre stage:

Team Name: Olympiakos Has Fallen
Reserves: Wolfsburg Of Wall Street
Youth Team: Palace In Wonderland
Stadium: Bernabeu After Reading

Management Team
Dead Poyets Society
12 Years A Slade
The Chronicles Of Hiddink

First Team

Dudek Where's My Carr	Shittu Shittu Bang Bang
Collateral Rammage	The Usual Busquets
The Neville Wears Prada	PS Mulumbu
Murty Dancing	Educating Lita
The Boy In The Striped	Amokachi If You Can
Olofinjanas (c)	Slumdog Aliadiere

Subs

Indiana Jones & The	The Hand That Rocks
Temple Of Poom	The Gradle
Who Framed Gary Mabbutt	Raging Bullard
The Mexes Chainsaw	Men Who Stare At Gotze
Massacre	No Country For Old
An Inconvenient Huth	Mendonca
Naked Gunter	

WINNING OVER FRIENDS TO FOOTBALL

Football has long been referred to as 'the beautiful game'. Many reading this would agree with that statement even though there are parts of it that are decidedly unattractive.

But there are some humans out there – as strange as it may seem – for whom the entire concept of football is beyond their comprehension. There are some people who have never heard of Ian Woan, Mark Pembridge and Chris Kiwomya. I have often wondered whether these sorts of individuals – heathens – can be won over to football once the finer points of the game are explained and the atmosphere of a match experienced.

A few seasons ago I conducted a football experiment on two young ladies called Libby and Sophie. The venue for this experiment was Hillsborough and the game was a classic Yorkshire derby pitting Sheffield Wednesday against Doncaster Rovers.

On the way to the ground we talked through the context of the encounter. I explained that Rovers were historically a lower-division side now playing in the Championship while Wednesday were once a 'big' club who spent too much in the 1990s and eventually paid the price. Both Libby and Sophie looked a little bored. I feared I had lost them already.

After we'd paid for our tickets, Sophie wondered where she'd be able to buy some pre-match tucker. I told her there would be a selection of reconstituted meats on offer at outrageous prices.

Libby had feared that would be the case and had come prepared... with a packed lunch.

Even my dad knows that packed lunches at football matches are a big no-no. He used to take an apple bag to every Crawley Town game, and I remember one Saturday he refused to give me 20p to buy a Marathon (now Snickers) at half time but was willing to offer me one of his Braeburns.

My issue with a packed lunch is that it robs you of one of the essential elements of the football experience – average food. A flask of tea or soup, if you're really cavalier, is acceptable but anything beyond that takes you into a dark place. You are a gingham cloth away from a game of polo!

Libby had brought the full selection. There were cheese sandwiches, crisps and a smattering of fresh fruit – all in individual Tupperware pots. I believe her visit constitutes the only time in history that a plum has been taken into Hillsborough.

Despite the odd looks from seasoned match-goers the ladies began to enjoy themselves. Once the game started there was a man behind us who kept shouting things like: 'Chuffing nut cakes Wens-dee' and 'Wens-dee... gerrit ont flu-er.' He really confused them when he accused Luke Varney of having a '50p head'.

'Sheffield aren't very good, are they?' offered Libby, ten minutes into the second half. 'You're not wrong, love,' came the response from nut-cake man, thankfully ignoring Libby's casual use of the generic 'Sheffield'.

When the seemingly inevitable Doncaster goal arrived I turned to see if the girls enjoyed it but they were facing the other way having their picture taken with some Chinese exchange students.

They were relieved at the final whistle, which was followed by another integral part of the football experience... staring at brake lights for the best part of an hour on the A61.

'So, did you enjoy that?' I proffered.

'Not really,' came a rather lukewarm response.

'Do you think you'll go to another one?' I asked tentatively. There was a long pause before the following reply: 'I've been now so I don't need to go again, do I?'

My experiment had failed. I watched Libby's face light up as she found another plum in her handbag. It was the happiest she'd been all night. There are some battles you just cannot win.

UNUSUAL OBJECTS SEEN AT FOOTBALL GROUNDS

My friend Libby's Tupperware-based packed lunch may have been weird but it was by no means the most unusual thing ever seen at a football ground.

A PIG'S HEAD

When world player of the year Luis Figo left Barcelona for hated rivals Real Madrid, his former fans had a surprise for him when he returned to play at the Nou Camp. As Figo went to take a corner, the severed head of a pig was hurled from the stands and landed at his feet. He brought home the bacon that day.

A BURNING SCOOTER

On their way to a home match against Atalanta, some rather enthusiastic Inter Milan fans stole a moped from an opposition supporter and smuggled – OK, wheeled – it into the San Siro with them. But they weren't done yet. They then set it on fire and tried to toss it from the second tier down to the pitch, but fortunately it only made it down to the empty lower tier.

MARS BARS

They may not have been pigs' heads, but scorned Newcastle fans on the Gallowgate End made their feelings about former idol Paul Gascoigne's weight very clear when they pelted him with frozen Mars bars (available outside the ground) on his return to St James' Park with Spurs. Just for good measure, Middlesbrough fans repeated the trick when the Gazza roadshow rolled into their corner of the North-east.

TENNIS BALLS

If a tennis ball protest works once, then do it again. Hull fans made their displeasure at owner and former tennis player and tennis club pioneer David Lloyd known by hurling hundreds of balls on to the pitch at an away game against Bolton. Meanwhile, over in Switzerland, fans of Basel and Lucerne did the same to make their anger felt over their televised match's kick-off time being brought forward so that a Roger Federer match could also be screened live.

A PARROT

A Hertfordshire Senior Centenary Trophy tie was delayed when 63-year-old Irene Kerrigan and her caged pet parrot were asked to leave the ground due to the disruption caused by the bird's ability to mimic the referee's whistle. 'Every time I blew my whistle the bird made exactly the same sound,' said referee Gary Bailey. 'It was bizarre. The crowd were all laughing. In the end, there was only one thing for it.'

A 38DD BRA

While all at Parkhead were celebrating Celtic's 44th Scottish Premier League title in 2013 by jumping up and down, singing and all those other things football fans do, one woman performed her own unique celebration. 'Superfan' Jan Upex marked the occasion by flinging her large brassiere on to the pitch instead. She was strangely able to give her full support without full support.

A HAND GRENADE

Fearless Scottish goalkeeper Chic Brodie was prepared for anything that came his way when Brentford played Millwall at Griffin Park in 1964. Unfortunately, he couldn't stop his team going down 2-1 to the Lions, whose fans threw a hand grenade into Chic's penalty area after their team's equalising goal. Brodie picked up the grenade and had a close look at it before nonchalantly chucking it into his goal. A policeman (PC Pat O'Connell, if you must know) carefully placed it into a bucket of sand before it was later discovered to be a harmless fake.

DOUGHNUTS

It seems an awful waste that would've left Homer Simpson requiring counselling for post-traumatic stress, but angry Hajduk Split fans in Croatia covered their pitch in doughnuts as part of a protest against their bakery-owning president.

HANDCUFFS

While certain footballers may not be strangers to handcuffs off the pitch, none of them expect to see a pair on it. But a goalless Everton v Manchester City Premier League game in 2012 was halted for five minutes when fan John Foley decided to handcuff himself to a Goodison Park goalpost in protest at Ryanair. The game was held up until a pair of bolt cutters were found, at which point the entertainment ended and fans had to start watching the match again.

SEX STUFF

Boca Juniors fans are passionate. So passionate that they bring dildos to matches with them. And they used them to take revenge on their former goalkeeper Montoya Navarro, who had the nerve to celebrate a win over Boca with his new club Independiente, and was subsequently attacked by the sex toys thrown from the stands.

UNLIKELY FOOTBALL FANS

Despite their lack of focus on the game, not to mention that packed lunch again, Libby and Sophie were by no means the most unlikely football fans I've ever seen. Far from it, judging by this lot of hangers-on.

SYLVESTER STALLONE (EVERTON)

Stallone's football pedigree is second to none, having performed heroics in goal in *Escape to Victory*. So it was no surprise when he turned up on the Goodison Park pitch for a home game against Reading, holding a scarf to the fans as if he'd done that sort of thing all his life.

MIKE TYSON (PETERBOROUGH UNITED)

Iron Mike could choose to support any team and nobody would argue with him. And nobody did when he strolled around the London Road pitch in a Posh shirt at half time of a 2010 friendly against West Ham, becoming a fan for life in the process.

Would you make a joke at the expense of this man? Neither would I

CAMERON DIAZ (BRENTFORD)

There have been no confirmed sightings of the Hollywood star at Griffin Park, but that doesn't mean she's not a huge Bees fan. According to former Brentford chairman Dan Tana, the actress was a regular at his Hollywood restaurant and always asked after the team. That is more than enough for us.

OSAMA BIN LADEN (ARSENAL)

The former al-Qaeda gaffer was a regular at Highbury while living in London, watching their run to the 1994 Cup Winners' Cup final. And, according to biographer Adam Robinson, he even bought his son Abdullah an Ian Wright replica shirt.

DALAI LAMA (BRADFORD CITY)

It's no coincidence that the 14th Dalai Lama sports claret-and-amber robes when he goes about his daily business. Those colours also happen to be the same as Bradford City's. Not only is his, er, holiness the honorary president of the team's fans' group, Friends of Bradford City (and he has the shirt to prove it), but he also sent the club a message blessing them ahead of their incredible appearance in the 2013 League Cup final.

DANIEL DAY-LEWIS (MILLWALL)

The Oscar-winning 'method' actor grew up in south-east London and spent his teenage years on the terraces at the Den, which inspired his acting in *Gangs of New York*: 'I remembered the days of fighting on the Millwall terraces and they stood me in good stead for Bill the Butcher,' he said.

KELSEY GRAMMER (EBBSFLEET OR BRISTOL ROVERS)

The man who played Frasier and, more importantly, voiced Sideshow Bob in *The Simpsons* became a fan of Ebbsfleet when they signed striker Phil Walsh – he had no choice because he's married to Phil's sister, actress Kayte Walsh. But, there may be a clash of loyalties because his wife's father, Alan, is the youth-team coach at Bristol Rovers and in 2014 the actor turned up and smiled a lot at their 2-1 defeat to Rochdale. He has a big decision to make because, as I explained to Libby and Sophie, you can't have any of this two-team rubbish.

RIDLEY SCOTT (HARTLEPOOL)

The *Blade Runner* director was born in South Shields, but wasn't interested in the North-east's fancy clubs. He studied at West Hartlepool College of Art and clearly paid the odd visit to Victoria Park, where he fell in love with the Monkey Hangers.

ANDREW LLOYD WEBBER (LEYTON ORIENT)

The Os were a showbiz club in the 1960s with West End impresarios Harry Zussman and Leslie Grade on the board, which must have stirred something in the musical maestro (and his cellist brother Julian) who is a big Orient fan.

ZAC EFRON (ARSENAL)

The *High School Musical* bloke came on *Football Focus* in 2014 claiming to be a fan of the Gunners. Upon further probing it became clear that if you asked him where the Clock End was he'd point cautiously to his wrist. He was 'taken' to one game; he couldn't remember who Arsenal played or what the score was. To complete the foolishness he described the entire experience as 'rad'. That, my friends, is the verbal equivalent of individual Tupperware.

POPE BENEDICT XVI (BAYERN MUNICH)

Joseph Ratzinger was born in a Bavarian town 70 miles away from Munich, but grew up supporting the club, who offered him honorary membership... when he became the Pope, not while he was growing up.

THE BEST DERBIES YOU'VE PROBABLY NEVER HEARD OF

Now you may not think Sheffield Wednesday v Doncaster Rovers is a great rivalry but in South Yorkshire, it matters – at least to the Rovers fans anyway. Here are a load of lesser-known, but no less fiercely contested, football rivalries.

MOHUN BAGAN v EAST BENGAL

Which sport would you guess holds the Indian stadium attendance record with a figure of 131,781? Amazingly enough, it's not cricket but football and all those people turned up to see the Kolkata derby in July 1997. East Bengal supporters usually have Bangladeshi ancestry while Mohun Bagan fans tend to originate from the part of Bengal which is now Indian. The fans have their own distinct ways of celebrating derby success, with the East Bengal fans dining out on hilsa fish if they win and their rivals opting for prawns. Which makes a pleasant change from copious amounts of beer.

AMERICA DE CALI v DEPORTIVO CALI

The Cauca Valley Clasico is Colombian football's fiercest rivalry between two teams that have won more than 20 league titles between them. It dates back to the first recorded meeting of the clubs in 1931 when Deportivo won 2-1, but America claimed both their opponents' goals were offside and that the referee had been bribed – and that therefore they had won 1-0. America's protests saw them banned for a year and the rivalry has simmered ever since.

ASANTE KOTOKO v HEARTS OF OAK

The biggest game in Ghanaian football is between Hearts of Oak, who hail from capital Accra, and Asante Kotoko, playing out of Ghana's second city Kumasi. The teams have dominated domestic football with more than 40 titles between them and enjoy a healthy and feisty rivalry, which will unfortunately always be overshadowed by the stadium disaster at the end of a 2001 derby which claimed 127 lives.

THE STRONGEST v BOLIVAR

This derby has been included mainly to point out that there is a Bolivian side called The Strongest. When the club was launched, it was the fashion to name teams in English, hence the unusual name. A few years later, another club sprung up in capital La Paz with an altogether more local name, Bolivar, and a rivalry was born.

AUSTRIA VIENNA v RAPID VIENNA

A simmering city rivalry steeped in bitterness and second only to Glasgow in its historical beginnings. Rapid are the working-class man's club compared to bourgeois Austria, whose early club statutes included a minimal intelligence requirement for players. One famous match between the clubs in 1937 saw the game abandoned after 80 minutes with Austria 5-0 ahead, as Rapid only had five outfield players remaining due to a combination of red cards and injuries.

ESTEGHLAL TEHRAN v PIROUZI TEHRAN

The Surkhabi derby is the biggest match in Iranian, if not Asian, football. When the Tehran powerhouses lock horns, the whole country gets involved, often with tragic consequences: in 2002 a 20-year-old was killed in a fight in south-west Iran after Pirouzi won the league. Two Tehran Club Championship matches between the sides in the 1970s were abandoned amid chaotic scenes and foreign referees took over the officiating after claims of domestic referee bias caused yet more controversy.

WISLA KRAKOW v CRACOVIA KRAKOW

Not wishing to overstate itself, the Krakow derby is known as the 'holy war'. The re-emergence of Cracovia as a football force relit the spark behind this city hatred and the rivalry exploded in the early 1990s when street fights saw Cracovia fans use knives and axes on their rivals, who reciprocated in kind. The atmosphere has been edgy ever since.

WREXHAM v CHESTER

It may not have the fame of the nearby Manchester and Merseyside derbies, but this rivalry is as intense as any across the globe. Two teams separated by 11 miles and two nationalities, whose fans loathe each other. In 2013, the clubs' first meeting in years saw violence flare after Wrexham fans held aloft banners mocking the deaths of two Chester fans. Chester supporters then began ripping out seats.

BLACKPOOL v PRESTON

Its roots might lie in a rather ancient era of English football when these two teams were the Liverpool and Manchester United North-west giants of their time, but it's no less intense these days. When Preston were relegated from the Championship in 2011, Blackpool fans sent over a light aircraft with two messages. The first said: 'We Are Superior – Love Blackpool FC', and the plane returned to say 'Poor Little Preston – Enjoy League 1'. The stunt prompted North End boss Phil Brown to say, 'Seriously, if I had a gun I would have shot the plane down.'

ORLANDO PIRATES v KAIZER CHIEFS

Imagine if Manchester City had been formed by a disgruntled former Manchester United player. That's pretty much what you have with the Soweto derby as Orlando Pirates fans have never forgiven their former player, Kaizer Motaung, for leaving them to play in North America, then returning to set up his own club – the Kaizer Chiefs. Recent highlights include a 12-man brawl in 2013.

The Soweto derby: a tad lively

How the Mighty Have Fallen

Sheffield Wednesday might have fallen on hard times but that was nothing compared to these former top-flight stars who wound up putting their boots on alongside everyday folk like you and me, in the non-League scene.

Pascal Chimbonda

The defender may have been on the bench for France at the 2006 World Cup final, but seven years later he turned out for Evo-Stik League South side Market Drayton in a pre-season friendly.

Paolo Vernazza

The one-time Arsenal starlet, who made a Champions League appearance for the Gunners, ended up doing a tour of the southern non-League scene, playing for Woking, Grays Athletic, Hemel Hempstead Town and Bishop's Stortford before calling it a day.

Jason Lee

As well as suffering the ignominy of having his 'pineapple' hair ridiculed on *Fantasy Football* every week in the 1990s, Lee also went from Premier League poacher with Nottingham Forest to non-League no-mark at Southern League Corby Town.

Trevor Benjamin

Peter Taylor paid £1.3 million to bring Benjamin from Cambridge to Premier League Leicester, but a few years later the bulky striker began an incredible journey through non-League, turning out for clubs including Wroxham, Bedlington Terriers and, finally, Seaton Delaval Amateurs in the Northern Alliance.

Dmitri Kharine

Before Roman Abramovich's roubles transformed Chelsea, his compatriot Kharine appeared between the Stamford Bridge sticks, playing in the FA Cup final along the way. It wasn't long before Dmitri swapped the King's Road for the, er, high street, at Conference South side Hornchurch – where he was sent off on his debut.

Christopher Wreh

The Liberian striker scored the winner in Arsenal's 1998 FA Cup semi-final against Wolves to help them to the double, but just five years later he lined up for Conference South side Bishop's Stortford, otherwise known as the 'Blue Brazil'.

Edgar Davids

The Dutchman tasted Champions League glory with Ajax in 1995 and reached a World Cup semi-final with Holland in 1998 but he bizarrely finished his career as player-manager of Conference side Barnet.

Socrates

Captaining Brazil at two World Cups didn't go to Socrates' head, which he proved by turning out for Northern Counties East League side Garforth Town in 2004.

Chris Waddle

England's World Cup wing wonder might have made the semi-finals of Italia 90 (and missed *that* penalty) but his last proper stint was with Northern Premier League side Worksop Town, where he was still playing into his forties.

George Best

The first rock 'n' roll footballer may have won the European Cup with Manchester United in 1968, but just six years later he made three appearances for Southern League Dunstable Town, managed by Barry Fry.

A far colder than usual Socrates

FAST FOOD XI

Libby and Sophie both brought some random items into Hillsborough but we all know that football culture is all about a celebration of rubbish food. The Fast Food XI does exactly that:

Team Name: KFC Wimbledon
Reserves: Dim-Sunderland
Youth Team: MSG Eindhoven
Stadium: Burgerbeu
Training Ground: Finger Lickin' Goodison

Management Team
Sillett-O-Fish
PoppaDomadoni

First Team

Brad Friedelivery	Hamann Pineapple
Drive Pugh	Mustapha Bhaji
Celestine Kebabayaro	Smicer Hut
Didier Pakora	Big Chamakh
Mushy Pienaars	Benteke Fried Chicken
Colonel Sanders Limpar (c)	

Subs

Sushi Jaaskelainen	Onion Frings
Landon DonnerVan	Victor Wagamama
Burrito Carbone	ChowMein Pennant

PEOPLE WITH PRESENCE

There are some people who have it. You know what I mean, the people who walk into a room and everyone feels compelled to look at them. They have that aura, swagger, confidence that mean all eyes are strangely drawn in their general direction.

I've interviewed Tiger Woods on a number of occasions and the build-up is always the same. There is always a nervous tension in the room before he arrives and his 'people' will walk in first to make sure all is well, check for exits and all that sort of stuff. Then there is a moment of hush when Woods himself enters the room and something definitely happens when he walks in. It may well be down to the bodyguards, agents and entourage but the man has something about him.

Cristiano Ronaldo has the same sort of presence about him and much of that is down to the fact that, when you meet him for the first time, he is much taller than you imagine and appears to be chiselled out of solid rock.

A few years ago I sat down with another footballer who, like Ronaldo, always leaves a mark. Eric Cantona had just been signed up as an ambassador for Umbro and I was called and asked whether I wanted to speak to him. He'd been off the radar for a while and when we were told the interview would be in New York, where Cantona was the new

A rare smile from the man who never gives anything away

director of football at the re-formed NY Cosmos, we jumped at the opportunity.

The interview involved something of a *Dirty Dozen*-style raid on New York. Lee Marvin wasn't involved but it was very much in and out in a few hours. We had arranged a meeting point in a swanky SoHo hotel but the term 'Looking for Eric' took on an entirely different meaning as the hours of waiting ticked by. Various members of Team Cosmos assured us he was coming and that we were very important to him.

When the door to a hotel room eventually opened, in walked the Frenchman wearing a flat cap and Cosmos jacket and looking a little like a slightly upmarket Zack Dingle. Strangely, he was holding a big apple and, with his legs planted unnecessarily wide apart, he took a giant bite out of his significant fruit and said, *'Bonjour.* I shall return in fifteen minutes.'

For you to fully appreciate the size of the apple I can tell you that when he did return – 25 minutes later – he still hadn't polished it off. Just before we started, I asked him if he would be wearing his hat for the whole interview. 'Of course,' he announced with a dismissive Gallic stare questioning how an Englishman could possibly doubt French fashion.

I had spoken to him a few times before but he seemed far more relaxed on this occasion – and slightly mischievous. He called the kung-fu kick at Selhurst Park in 1995 the highlight of his career and spoke about being a 'prisoner of his memories'. There was a telling look on his face that said 'that's your story there, young man'.

At one point he stood up and started taking his microphone off. I asked him what he was doing and he said it felt 'like a good point to finish'. I laughed and asked him to sit back down. After yet another apple, thankfully he agreed.

The interview lasted just short of an hour. He smiled, stood up, thanked everyone in the room and left, picking up – you've guessed it – another apple on his way out. One of his entourage came back and said that 'the biggest compliment I can pay you is that I think he quite enjoyed it'.

When we put the interview out the following weekend it made headlines in all the papers, crashed the New York Cosmos website and was the sixth most-tweeted video in the world.

Whatever it is, Cantona has got it – and lots of it.

ARTY FOOTBALLERS À LA ERIC

Reinventing himself as some kind of philosopher and actor after his football career was another stroke of Cantona genius. But our Eric isn't the only round-ball clogger who can claim to have an arty side.

JODY CRADDOCK

Not only was Jody a fine centre-back for both Sunderland and Wolves, but he was also a ridiculously talented artist, specialising in landscapes and contemporary portraits. His work has featured in exhibitions, rarely sells for less than £500 a pop, and he did a great line in famous footballer portraits too. Really.

JOEY BARTON

There was a spell when the outspoken midfielder used his Twitter account to convince his followers that he was a deep philosophical thinker. He regularly quoted Nietzsche, Virgil and Aristotle. It wasn't a wind-up. Joseph soon embarked on a philosophy degree at Roehampton University.

GRAEME LE SAUX

In Graeme's day, merely reading the *Guardian* was enough to set him apart from his Chelsea team-mates and make him a cultural outsider. But, on top of that, the left-back also eschewed the pub for the cafe and enjoyed visiting art galleries – all of which led his colleagues to describe him as a bit avant-garde. Or words to that effect.

ANTON FERDINAND

The defender has a softer side as he's a fairly accomplished singer, piano player and drum, er, beater. As a child, Anton also enjoyed horse riding but wasn't allowed to indulge himself during his career. 'I don't own any horses but I still go to the stables that I went to,' he says. 'I still go there a lot. It's something different, where I can get away from everything. I enjoy being around the people there and sometimes I help out with the horses. The one thing I would like to do is ride but I can't do that. I will when my career is over.'

NOLBERTO SOLANO

The Peruvian Geordie was a rather accomplished trumpet player and used to wind up his manager, the late great Sir Bobby Robson, by phoning him up and playing the trumpet. 'He didn't know it was me,' says Nobby, 'but one day somebody told him that I knew how to play the trumpet. So then he worked out that it must be me. He called me up and just laughed with me down the phone.'

DANIEL AGGER

The Danish defender is covered from his neck to his ankle in tatts, but also happens to be a qualified tattoo artist. He has repeatedly offered to tattoo his Liverpool team-mates for free should they land the Premier League title – which might explain the Reds' persistent failure to do so.

DAVID JAMES

Like Jody Craddock, the goalkeeper is something of an artist, who has produced several paintings. He also illustrated a children's book for a colleague at Portsmouth, called *Harry's Magic Pockets* which has nothing to do with Mr Redknapp. 'It is about a boy called Harry who transports his friend Teigan to the circus by delving into his enchanted pocket,' explained James.

PAUL SCHARNER

The former Wigan and West Brom star was partial to a bit of classical music in his spare time, bucking the trend for most R&B-loving footballers. 'Mozart brings me down,' he says. 'He takes me away from football. I spend time imagining how he pieces his music together. I wonder how it is possible to think that big, to bring together the violins and wind instruments. It's good for brain development. And there is a connection. I believe Mozart was very strong, mentally.'

Press Conference Gold: The Managers Who Held a Room For All the Wrong Reasons

Very few are able to hold a room like Cantona, but there are several managers who can command the attention of a pack of journalists with some choice words. So here are my favourite press conferences where the gaffers lost it.

Rafa Benitez I

In 2009, the boss of top-of-the-table Liverpool had finally had enough of Sir Alex Ferguson and prepared a press conference diatribe. I was at Melwood that day and from the moment the door opened and the Spaniard walked in you could tell there was something he wanted to get off his chest. Rafa took his seat and listed a series of, what he considered to be, indisputable facts: 'I was surprised by what has been said, but maybe they [Manchester United] are nervous because we are at the top of the table. But I want to talk about facts. I want to be clear, I do not want to play mind games too early, although they seem to want to start. But I have seen some facts.'

Rafa went on to read out an exhaustive list of complaints about Fergie's conduct with referees and perceived fixture list injustice, adding: 'There is another option. That Mr Ferguson organises the fixtures in his office and sends it to us and everyone will know and cannot complain. That is simple.'

To this day Mr Benitez has continued to claim it wasn't a 'rant', but Manchester United went on to win the title.

Rafa Benitez II

It's fair to say that Rafa Benitez's appointment as Chelsea's interim manager didn't go down too well with the club's fans, who hadn't forgiven him for his 'plastic flag' comments when he was Liverpool manager. He'd suggested that Liverpool fans didn't need help to make an atmosphere like Chelsea fans did with their accessories, and he was never made to feel welcome at Stamford Bridge. In fact, he faced outright hostility and after an FA Cup tie at Middlesbrough one night, he said: 'I've been in charge of football for twenty-six years. I've won the Champions League, FA Cup, Italian Super Cup, Spanish league twice. Nine trophies, all the trophies you can win at club level. But there is a group of fans who are not doing the team any favours. They are singing and wasting time preparing banners and it is because someone made a mistake. They put my title "interim manager!" and I'll leave at the end of the season, so they don't need to waste time with me. That group is not doing the club, the players or the other fans any favours. What they have to do is continue supporting the team. If we cannot achieve what we expect to achieve, to be in the top four and be in the Champions League next year, I will leave.

'The club will stay in the Europa League but the fans will have to take responsibility too. The fans put the players under pressure and they do not create a good atmosphere at Stamford Bridge. They have to realise they are making a big mistake as the rest of the fans want to see the team in the Champions League next year. It would be better for everyone to have a good atmosphere, supporting the team – that's it.'

Joe Kinnear

If we're talking press conference gold, then you really can't look any further than Newcastle's Joe Kinnear, whose foul-mouthed, expletive-laden performance in front of shocked North-east football correspondents remains the standard-bearer for all public rants. As this is a family book, much of what Joe said remains unprintable. Suffice to say he was far from happy with his treatment by reporters and told them so by swearing at them repeatedly. In one of his cleaner outbursts he felt he was being victimised: 'I ain't coming up here to have the p**s taken out of me,' he said. 'I have a million pages of crap that has been written about me. I'm ridiculed for no reason. I'm defenceless. I can't get a point in, I can't say nothing, I can't do nothing, but I ain't going to be negative.'

And if not being negative is breaking all previously known swearing world records and being thoroughly offensive, then Joe was true to his word.

David Moyes

The former Everton manager found a unique way to hold the attention of a room when he attended a pre-match Toffees press conference and kept quiet in 2009. Moyes had been happily talking about the forthcoming Bolton game when he was asked about an alleged training-ground bust-up with Victor Anichebe. His answer was total silence. Despite several attempts at follow-up questions on other subjects, Moyes continued to keep quiet until the club's press officer called a halt to proceedings.

Javier Clemente

The Athletic Bilbao coach was briefing the press when he became embroiled in a spat with a reporter. The journalist insisted he had every right to his opinion as he'd watched so much football, to which Clemente replied: 'The cows at Lezama [Athletic Bilbao's countryside training ground] watch football every day and they haven't got a f*****g clue.'

Christian Gross

The journo pack assembled at White Hart Lane for the unveiling of Tottenham's new manager in 1997 were kept waiting as the new man was late. This was Spurs' answer to Arsenal's Arsene Wenger – nobody had known much about him either but he was about to embark on a period of extraordinary success for the club. Sadly for Gross, he was not. He finally arrived and it soon became clear why he had been delayed, as he produced a tube ticket from his top pocket and said: 'This is my Underground ticket. I came like the normal people come to the football club. I travelled like the normal people on the Underground. That is how I came to Tottenham. I want this to become my ticket to dreams.'

A top-level boardroom meeting... no one got fired

The room fell silent. Spurs chairman Alan Sugar looked shocked, and later wrote in his autobiography: 'I knew from that moment that Gross was dead meat.'

Jose Mourinho

The Portuguese prince of press conferences knows how to hold a room, and set his stall out with an unforgettable performance upon his introduction to the British media when he took over at Chelsea in 2004, fresh from winning the Champions League with Porto: 'Please don't call me arrogant, but I'm European champion and I think I'm a special one. We have top players and, sorry if I'm arrogant, we have a top manager.'

Sir Alex Ferguson

The list of the times Fergie's presence filled a packed press room with fear is far too long to be featured in its entirety here, but arguably his most memorable encounter with the Fourth Estate came when he was under pressure and facing a trophy-less season in 2002. Much attention had been focused on the performances of star signing Juan Sebastian Veron, and Fergie's patience finally snapped. 'Yous are all f*****g idiots,' he barked in Joe Kinnear style. 'He's a f*****g great player. Get out!' And promptly ordered all the assembled hacks off the premises.

Seeing red: interviewing Sir Alex

Avram Grant

The Chelsea manager had just seen his side beat Everton to stay on the coat-tails (not that anyone wears those any more) of Manchester United in the 2007/08 title race, but he wasn't happy. So he decided not to play ball at the post-match press conference, by delivering monosyllabic answers. Like this:

A deserved win Avram?
'Yes.'

What particularly pleased you about the performance?
'I'm pleased.'

What in particular pleased you?
(after an eight-second delay) 'I don't know.'

Is it a relief to win here?
'Yes.'

You seem lost for words by the performance. Are you more satisfied with the performance or the victory?
'Both.'

It went on for a further five minutes, until he was asked about injuries to his players:

Did Michael Essien faint?
'He had some problems, but he is OK.'

Michael Ballack?
'Injured.'

What's his problem?
'Ask the doctor.'

He's not here!
'Well, call him then.'

Have you ever played the yes-no game, Avram?
Chelsea press officer: 'This is going nowhere. Let's end it.'

Not Every Football Partnership Is As Cool As Cantona and the Cosmos

With Eric the King, and their retro 1970s vibe, the New York Cosmos were on to a good thing, but not all football partnerships can be as cool as that one. Especially in this global age of corporate sponsorship, there are some pretty unusual ones out there.

CLYDEBANK AND WET WET WET

The former Scottish League team signed up to a deal with local hero Marti Pellow and his fellow band members, and wore the group's name on their shirts in the mid-1990s. Moist madness.

LIVERPOOL AND GARUDA INDONESIA

You what? Garuda is the national airline of Indonesia, of course, and given how many Liverpool fans populate the South-east Asian nation it made perfect sense for them to sponsor Liverpool's training kit.

MANCHESTER UNITED AND MISTER POTATO

The last time I checked, Mr Potato was a cult TV figure but apparently he's also the official savoury snack partner – or packet of crisps to you and me – of the Old Trafford club. What's more, Wayne Rooney was roped in to be the official face of Mister Potato. You can do the rest for yourself.

VOUKEFALA AND SOULA

The Greek amateurs were struggling for cash in 2012, so when Soula, the local brothel, made them an offer they couldn't refuse, they shook hands furiously. Club president Giannis Batziolas joked: 'When we announced to the players that our sponsor would be a brothel, they wanted to know about bonuses.'

AC MILAN AND POOH

It was probably lost on the locals, but Milan's 1980/81 shirt was sponsored by jeans manufacturers Pooh, which means one of Europe's greatest clubs spent the season running around Serie A with Pooh on their shirts.

ARSENAL AND COOPER TIRE EUROPE

When the money men at Arsenal had a long look at their list of sponsors, they realised they'd completely forgotten to bring someone on board to be their official tyre partner – heads must have rolled over that cock-up. Fortunately, Cooper Tire Europe, who specialise in 4x4 and performance passenger tyres (and have spelling issues), were on hand to step in to become the 'Official Tyre of Arsenal Football Club' – but only in Europe, Russia, the Middle East, South Africa and selected North African countries, mind. The rest of the world is still an untapped rubber market.

SUNDERLAND AND NIP + MAN

Ever wondered why Paolo Di Canio and his Sunderland successor Gus Poyet always seemed to look immaculate, without a blemish on their faces? The answer is simple – the club have taken on Nip + Man as their official male grooming partner, meaning fans, players and management should be the best-looking in the league. In theory.

HULL AND BURFLEX SCAFFOLDING

Everyone needs a bit of scaffolding in their lives, especially football fans. But none need it more than the supporters of Hull City, who would've been delighted to find out that Burflex are an official partner of the Tigers, which will come in very handy for any ground improvements.

THE INTERVIEWS THAT COULD HAVE BEEN HANDLED A LITTLE BETTER

Not everyone in football is as professional as Monsieur Cantona who, despite one attempt to walk off, spent an age answering all of my questions. Not this lot, though – most of them could've done with taking a media training course or two.

HARRY REDKNAPP

Normally the most affable and generous manager with his time, Spurs manager Harry went off the rails when Sky Sports' Rob Palmer made an innocent joke he didn't like.

'You made your name as a wheeler and dealer,' began Rob, 'but there's not been much wheeling and dealing here, has there?'

'No, I'm not a wheeler-dealer, f*** off!'

Harry then walked off, but could be heard shouting in the background, 'Don't say that. I'm a f*****g football manager!'

Managed to get through this of without mentioning the 'w' or the 'd' word

RON ATKINSON

Big Ron was Coventry boss when he was being interviewed by Richard Keys and Andy Gray, who were both in the safety of the studio, after a defeat against relegation rivals Southampton. When it was suggested to him by Keys that the team needed to play better, he lashed out. 'I'm sorry, you can sit there and play with all your silly machines as much as you like,' he said to Keys and Gray. 'I'm the manager of the football team, an experienced manager. If the boys hadn't done enough I'll whip 'em, but I ain't whipping them for that tonight. Who won the man of the match award?'

'Dave Beasant,' said Keys, confirming it was the Southampton goalkeeper.

'Sorry, so we must have played not bad then,' replied Atkinson. 'Thank you very much, lads, see you later.'

And with that he hurled the giant headphones he'd been forced to wear for the interview across the room, accidentally whacking a Sky producer with them, before apologising – all in front of the live cameras.

WALTER SMITH

When, the morning after Rangers had lost at home to AEK Athens, BBC reporter Chick Young dared to suggest to the manager that new signings Basile Boli and Brian Laudrup had been 'big disappointments' for the club on the European stage and that he might need to spend more to compete in the Champions League, Smith hit the roof. 'How can you say that? They just came into the place and you've got to give everyone a chance to settle in. Are you saying Boli and Laudrup cannae play in Europe? Boli's got a European Cup winner's medal for f***'s sake, you can't say he's not a good enough player to play in Europe. That's f*****g stupid, innit?'

The attack continued with Smith incredulous at Young's line of questioning, completing his onslaught with the memorable: 'If we had a bad night last night, you're having a f*****g horrendous morning now!'

JIM MCLEAN

The former Dundee United manager was facing calls to resign as chairman of the board after a disastrous start to the season saw the club hit rock bottom – and McLean soon followed. Shortly after a 4-0 home defeat to Hearts, a crowd gathered outside Tannadice to protest against McLean, as he conducted an interview with the BBC's John Barnes (not that one). McLean stated, 'There is absolutely no way that I will walk away from this situation,' before Barnes asked him how long he would give the manager Alex Smith to get it right on the park.

'You think I'm gonnae answer a stupid question like that?' replied McLean.

'I'm only asking it,' said Barnes.

'I told you earlier I wouldn't be f*****g answering that – and make sure that's cut!' stormed McLean as he walked towards Barnes off camera, punched him in the mouth, and added: 'And I'll tell you something, don't f*****g ever offer me that again!'

Shortly after, McLean did indeed walk away from that situation forever as he resigned.

GEORGE BEST

When the alcoholic football legend appeared on BBC1's *Wogan* show, it was clear from the start that he was far from sober. Wogan himself said: 'I could see him coming at me from across the stage. The eyes are glazed and I knew the worst had happened. He'd shunted down several bucketfuls in about five minutes. So he comes across to me and he's as drunk as a skunk.'

The interview had to be cut short, but not before a giggling George had time to say: 'Terry, I like screwing, all right?'

'So what do you do with your time these days?' replied Wogan.

'Screw.'

CARLOS TEVEZ

The quiet Argentine never said much during his time in England, mainly due to the language barrier. But he wasn't afraid to make his feelings perfectly clear in Spanish after his Manchester City side had beaten former club Manchester United in the League Cup. Before the match, his ex-team-mate Gary Neville had claimed Tevez wasn't worth the £25 million it would have taken for United to keep him, mildly irking the striker, who directed his goal celebration in the match at Neville.

Talking to ESPN Argentina radio, Tevez said: 'My celebration was directed at Gary Neville. He acted like a complete sock-sucker [boot-licker] when he said I wasn't worth twenty-five million pounds, just to suck up to the manager. I don't know what the hell that idiot is talking about me for. I never said anything about him.

'I will never show a lack of respect towards anyone. Just as I was running off to celebrate the penalty I had scored, I came across Gary and I said to myself: "Shut your trap, keep quiet." I didn't go overboard in my celebration and it was directed at Gary, not at Ferguson and not at the fans. I think he did the wrong thing because I was his team-mate and I never said anything bad about him. He was saying that Ferguson was right when he said that I wasn't worth twenty-five million, when he was saying this and that ... I always respected Neville.'

DIEGO MARADONA

Unsurprisingly, the Hand of God merchant himself was known to have a post-match strop or two, but none was better than his reaction to his Argentina side's qualification for the 2010 World Cup after a hard-fought win over Uruguay. At the post-match press gathering, Maradona's first words to the assembled reporters were: 'You lot take it up the a**e. If the ladies will pardon the expression... certain people who have not supported me, and you know who you are, can keep sucking,' and as he said that, he grabbed his genitals with both hands and gestured towards the TV cameras.

KEVIN KEEGAN

Let's be honest, this section would be incomplete without King Kev's infamous outburst in front of the Sky cameras at the climax of the race for the 1996 Premier League. After Newcastle had beaten Leeds, Keegan decided to send a little message to his title rival Alex Ferguson, who had wound him up by suggesting teams would try harder against the Red Devils than they would against Newcastle. 'I've kept really quiet but I'll tell you something,' said Keegan, 'he went down in my estimation when he said that. We have not resorted to that. You can tell him now, we're still fighting for this title and he's got to go to Middlesbrough and get something. And I'll tell you, honestly, I will love it if we beat them. Love it... But it really has got to me. I've voiced it live, not in front of the press or anywhere. I'm not even going to the press conference. But the battle is still on and Man United have not won this yet.'

Except they had.

Military XI

Now I know there was only a fleeting reference to *The Dirty Dozen* earlier but that gives me the perfect excuse to throw in one of my favourite XIs... the ones who wear the combat trousers.

Team Name: Walkie Torquay
Reserves: Pistol City
Stadium: Valley Grenade

Management Team
Gestapo Poyet
Behind McMenemy Lines
D-Day Deschamps
Booby Trapattoni

First Team
Desert Vorm
Armoured Personnel Carragher
David MayK47
Black Gorkss Downing
Call Of Guti (c)
Bannan Fodder
LieuPennant
Territorial Barmby
World War Wanchope
World War Pugh
Dexter Blackops

Subs
Truce Grobbelaar

Philippe Surrenderos
Camp Bastion Schweinsteiger
SASien

Medel Of Honour
Pirlo Harbor
NapoLeon Osman

WHEN TWITTER GOES WRONG

Twitter is a wonderful tool for the footballer. Cristiano Ronaldo has about a bagillion followers and even those put off by the perils of social media are encouraged to use it by their 'people' in order to strengthen the 'brand'. It is how the watching world chooses to communicate and commentate and – despite the obvious immediacy and access it offers – it can equally be a cesspool of bile, vitriol and general hatred.

Some footballers use it wisely while others have found themselves thoroughly flummoxed by its confusing boundaries.

We shall look at some famous examples later in the chapter but here are my golden rules when it comes to using Twitter and social media. Footballers, take note.

- Never compare your boss, a team-mate or the Football Association to any sort of genitalia.
- Never Photoshop a referee even if your mate thinks it's 'well funny' or 'sick'.
- Never complain about not being picked.
- Never mention Liverpool in a tweet (unless you play for Liverpool).
- Never direct-message a young lady asking if she wants to 'hook up'.
- Never tweet a picture of your massive garage with cars in it that have a combined monetary value greater than your number of followers.

- If you want to move club it's probably not a good idea to slag off:
  a) your current club
  b) your future club
  c) your current director of football
  d) Daniel Levy.
- Under no circumstances should any member of your family – especially your partner – be allowed to tweet from your account, or indeed about you or your career at any stage.
- If all you ever do is respond to the haters... You will get more haters.
- Never engage in Twitter 'banter' with Piers Morgan.
- Never press the 'camera' button on your phone when you, or anyone you know, could be, in any way, considered 'naked'.

Social media gurus all go on about the 90:10 principle – that you should spend 10 per cent of your time creating content and 90 per cent of your time interacting with your clients or followers. The majority of footballers get the balance right these days but if the above rules are adhered to then almost nothing can go wrong. That said, there are times when genuine errors take place.

I once texted a friend: 'I'll see you on the 4th floor of the multi-storey car park at 10pm', but foolishly tweeted instead of texting it. I faced a day of accusations but even that didn't compare to a pre-Twitter 'incorrect text disaster' from a few years ago.

One football club had just appointed their first Head of Communications – a man by the name of Paddy. I was invited to meet him and diligently entered his details into my phone. My wife was, at the time, saved in my phone as 'Princess' so that when I pressed the 'P' button on my old-school Nokia, she popped straight up.

That evening I texted Sarah the following message: 'Hi love. Can't wait to see you later. It's been a long time.' Muscle-memory took me through the sending process and even though I clearly saw

'Paddy' rather than 'Princess' I couldn't prevent my thumb from hitting 'send'. I opted for the old turn-the-phone-off-immediately-and-hope-for-the-best technique but unfortunately that never works.

When I turned it back on, it was ringing immediately but with an unknown number. I answered tentatively...

'Who are you and why are you ringing my husband, bitch?' came the unexpectedly abrupt retort.

The lady on the other end, Paddy's wife, was a little surprised when a man apologised for an errant text and she quickly calmed down once I explained the issue and the fact that I had no amorous intent when it came to her other half. Thinking before you text, tweet or in fact do anything is a valuable life lesson for us all.

FOOTBALLERS' TWITTER FAUX PAS

So many footballers have fallen foul of the Twitter temptation to really go off on one. You could probably fill a book with them, but here are some wonderful examples of those careless keyboard warriors, in all their grammatical glory.

DARREN BENT

If you're not getting a game at Spurs and you really want chairman Daniel Levy to know that you want to move to Sunderland, there's only one way to go about it. Set up a meeting with the chairman? Of course not. You do it the Darren Bent way: 'Do I wanna go Hull City NO. Do I wanna go Stoke NO do I wanna go Sunderland YES so stop f***ing around levy.'

RYAN BABEL

When fans are peeved after a perceived injustice they take to social media and post silly pictures of referees wearing the opposition kit to vent their frustrations. That's not usually what players do, but that's exactly what Babel did after Liverpool's FA Cup defeat to Manchester United in which they also had a player sent off. The Dutchman was fined £10,000 by the FA for tweeting a picture of Howard Webb in a United shirt and writing: 'And they call him one of the best referees? That's a joke.'

ASHLEY COLE

The Chelsea player appeared as a witness in the FA Commission's investigation into the Anton Ferdinand and John Terry racism incident. But in their final report, the commission completely dismissed Cole's evidence. And he didn't take that lying down, picking up a £90,000 fine for the trouble of typing the following into his phone: 'Hahahahaa, well done #fa I lied did I, #BUNCHOFT***S.'

WAYNE ROONEY

It took a while for everyone to believe Wayne Rooney's Twitter account was genuine, but one tweet certainly made a strong case. The Manchester United star became involved in a spat with a troll who was goading him and delivered these thinly veiled threats to his nemesis: 'Haha you know where I train every day kid come and do it good luck.'

And: 'I'll put u asleep within 10 seconds u little girl. Don't say stuff and not follow up on it. I'll be waiting.'

WOJCIECH SZCZESNY I

The Arsenal goalkeeper probably thought he was being clever when he sent a text message to raunchy late-night channel Elite presenter Letesha Collins. But the model found out the Gunner had a girlfriend and decided to expose him by posting a picture of the text message she claimed he sent her on Twitter. It read: 'Hello babe a will-be glamour model. Text me on 0779xxxxxxxx if you wanna talk. Don't give this number to anyone pls x.'

WOJCIECH SZCZESNY II

When Aaron Ramsey posted on Twitter a picture of himself wearing a tank top and ready for a round of golf, he could hardly have expected his team-mate to respond with these two tweets:

'I don't wanna be rude mate but you look like a rapist on that picture! lol.'

And: 'Looking like a rapist/pedofile isn't a good thing either ;)'

Ramsey took the insult in good spirits but it wasn't long before the obligatory apology tweet from Szczesny was forthcoming: 'I'm sorry if anyone was offended by my previous tweets. There are some things we should not joke about and I have crossed the line. Sorry!'

NILE RANGER I

If there's one thing football fans definitely dislike – other than pretty much every referee ever – it's one of their own players criticising their support. Which is probably why Newcastle's Nile Ranger should have thought twice before sending out these FIVE tweets after a home defeat to Reading:

'Certain fans need to not come and support this team… Coming out to BOOO us… Stay at home… Don't need ur BOO's… SAY NO MORE !!!!'

'Last thing from me… To all the fans. U are not forced to buy season tickets… Or pay our wages… Please remember that…'

'If u are loyal fans… Be with us… When we are out there on the field… Be the 12th man.. Don't come and BOO… That aint going to help any1.'

'Team is going through rough patch… Last thing we need is fans against us #SIMPLEREALLY.'

'We are a TEAM u BOO 1 player… Ur booing all of us !!!'

NILE RANGER II

If Newcastle fans weren't already enraged by Ranger's tweets, he really put the boot in by posting an Instagram picture of his surname – not that offensive on the surface but when you consider he used £1,500 worth of £20 notes to spell his name out, you can be sure that the reaction was far from positive.

JOSE ENRIQUE

Staying at Newcastle, Jose Enrique was a little miffed at the club selling some of their best players and took to his phone to express his displeasure at the departures of Andy Carroll and Kevin Nolan (Nobby). But he expressed it so well that the club decided to fine him £100,000: 'The club is allowing all the major players of the team to go. Seriously, do you think it is the fault of the players? Andy, nobby etc etc.'

'This club will never again fight to be among the top 6 again with this policy.'

When fans began tweeting replies to him, he continued his overly honest assessment and revealed the club had offered him an unimproved contract: 'They give the money I have already. They lie all the time. But is no for money is because they don't want spend in the club and bring quality players that's why everybody go.'

MICHAEL CHOPRA

You know what it's like. You're a professional footballer and you turn up for training and things aren't exactly as they should be so you go and have a quiet word with the gaffer to find out what's going on... Oh no, hang on, that's not what you do. If you're Michael Chopra you take to Twitter to savage the way Blackpool trained one morning, and pick up a £10,000 fine for your trouble: 'F***ing joke this come in training only 6 f***ing players here then find out the fitness coach taken the football session #joke.'

JASON PUNCHEON

The Crystal Palace midfielder was taking some stick for missing a penalty at Spurs and deservedly so, because the ball he struck so high and wide has still not been found to this day. Puncheon rolled with the blows until he heard his former manager Neil Warnock wading in on talkSPORT: 'There's no way I would've trusted him with a penalty. You've got to have somebody a little bit more cool, and he's not like that, Jason. He can whack a thirty-five-yard free kick in here and there but a penalty, with all the pressure on him at a place like White Hart Lane – not in a million years for me.'

So Puncheon took the only course of action available to him with a Twitter attack on Warnock, which included these tweets: 'The fact he could even talk about training is shocking he was never there...'

'Everything else is banter and opinions and as a man I will live with that which is fine but I will not live with his opinion.'

WHEN FOOTBALL AND TECHNOLOGY IS A TOTAL DISASTER

Smartphones, computers and the like have definitely enhanced our enjoyment of the beautiful game more than ever before. But, occasionally, technology and football are not such happy bedfellows...

DAVID JAMES'S COMPUTER GAMES

That might sound like the name of a *Viz* cartoon, but the former Liverpool goalkeeper once blamed a series of costly blunders for the Anfield club on the fact that he'd been staying up late at night playing computer games.

LEYTON ORIENT'S *FIFA 14* FAILURE

James wasn't the only one who suffered from overdoing it on the PlayStation. Leyton Orient, early League 1 pacesetters in 2013/14, suffered a sudden blip after winning their first eight games, with the blame firmly going on the players' addiction to the new *FIFA 14* game. '[The players] got stuck into the new *FIFA 14* game and at times even played as themselves against Oldham in preparation for the match the following day,' said a club spokesman, after Orient drew that match. 'The staff were quick to implement a "no *FIFA* on a match day" rule, however. The gaffer suspects several hours' playing football on a video game is not conducive to a good performance in the real thing.'

RIO FERDINAND'S TV TRAUMA

While playing for Leeds, the defender was relaxing at home, watching television with his foot up on the coffee table. Nothing to report here, right? Wrong. Ferdinand managed to strain a tendon behind his knee due to the way he was sitting.

CRISTIANO RONALDO'S CAR WRECK

Give a young footballer a load of money and he will inevitably blow a good part of it on an incredible supercar – the only problem being that supercars and footballers don't always get on that well. The man who would go on to win World Player of the Year (eventually), was driving his £150,000 Ferrari in a tunnel near Manchester airport when he somehow smashed it into a metal barrier, totalling it in the process.

NORTH KOREA'S FLAG DISASTER

Big screens, Jumbotrons, call them what you like – most people would agree they're a great addition to the match-day experience. Most people that is, except anyone from North Korea. Lining up for their Olympic women's football match against Colombia at Hampden Park one evening in 2012, the North Koreans were horrified to see their players being displayed on the big screen alongside the flag of bitter enemies South Korea, and promptly walked off the pitch in protest. After a delay of more than an hour to sort out the technical glitch, the match eventually kicked off. And the North Koreans won 2-0. Point made.

KIRK BROADFOOT'S MICROWAVE MELTDOWN

The Rangers full-back was already out injured with a foot injury when things got a whole lot worse. Broadfoot was inspecting two poached eggs he'd just microwaved when one of them exploded in his face, scalding him with hot water. Ouch.

MARIO BALOTELLI'S FIREWORKS FLOP

It's the weekend of the Manchester derby – in which you're playing – and you're bored at home late on Friday night, so what do you do? Let off some fireworks, of course. No major problem in that unless those fireworks are let off inside your house.

Unfortunately for Mario, that's what happened, as he and four friends began lighting fireworks from his first-floor bathroom window. Naturally, one of those fireworks set some bathroom towels on fire and the blaze spread until ten firefighters were on the scene dealing with what they described as 'a substantial fire' at Mario's Cheshire home. Oops.

DARIUS VASSELL'S POWER DRILL PERIL

The former Aston Villa striker was suffering with a swollen toe so tried to relieve the pressure, as you do, by drilling through his toenail with a power drill. As you don't. Vassell's toe got infected and he missed several games.

GARRY COOK'S EMAIL BOMBSHELL

We've all done it. Sent an email and included the wrong person on it by mistake – a reply-all instead of a reply, if you will. But I'm not sure many of us will have mocked the person we erroneously included for having cancer. That was the fate which befell Manchester City chief executive Garry Cook and cost him his job. The club were locked in a contract dispute with Nedum Onuoha and his mother, who had been suffering with cancer, and she'd explained as much in an email.

Inexplicably, Cook decided to mock her for her comment that she was 'ravaged with it' in an email to the club's football administrator Brian Marwood, with whom he used to work at Nike: 'Ravaged with it!! ... I don't know how you sleep at night. You used to be such a nice man when I worked with you at Nike,' he wrote.

Unfortunately for Cook, Mrs O also received the email and the rest is history – as was Cook.

MAROUANE FELLAINI'S MOBILE MADNESS

These days, we're all tied to our phones to a degree but most of us know when it's inappropriate to use them – funerals and while presenting TV programmes are generally accepted as major no-no's. But Marouane Fellaini must have taken temporary leave of his senses when he took his phone with him to the Manchester United bench for a home game against Newcastle, and was subsequently pictured absorbed by his phone rather than the spectacle in front of him. Which was probably understandable as his side struggled to a 1-0 defeat.

NEYMAR'S PHONE FANS

Sticking with mobile phones, the Brazilian superstar must regret the invention of the clever little things, such is the devotion of his fans to staying in touch with him. The poor guy has to regularly change his number due to the incessant calls and texts from fans at all hours of the day and night. 'I am unable to keep the same number for more than two weeks because people who call themselves fans – Neymarzetes – call me in the early hours of the morning or send me messages,' he says. 'And worse they discover the numbers of my family, girlfriend and friends and they invent stories and tell lies so that in the end they also have to change their numbers.'

MANAGERS' SACKING SURPRISES

Over the years, there's been no shortage of technology available to sack managers in the most dastardly ways, rather than just telling them to their faces. In the pre-internet era, Bobby Robson discovered he'd been given the elbow by Fulham when he walked past an *Evening Standard* placard outside Putney train station which read: 'Robson Sacked'.

Then, in 1997, Bruce Rioch was QPR manager until he read on Ceefax that he'd been sacked – at which point he wasn't QPR manager any more.

More recently, Gus Poyet was working on the BBC's Confederations Cup coverage as a studio guest when a print-out of a statement posted on the Brighton & Hove Albion website was handed to him, which confirmed he was leaving the club – it was the first he'd heard of it.

But perhaps, best – no, actually worst – of all was the way Sakaryaspor boss Saban Yildirim was fired. The Turkish club's manager was a guest on a live TV phone-in programme when he fielded a call from Cihan Yildiran, a club board member: 'Saban humiliated the club, so he is removed,' said Yildiran. And that was that.

WHEN FOOTBALL AND TECHNOLOGY IS A MARRIAGE MADE IN HEAVEN

But, of course, it isn't just bad news when football and technology collide. For every daft online petition to ban Tom Cleverley from the World Cup finals, there's a heartwarming story of social media rallying round to help a stricken footballer – OK, not exactly, but these wonderful examples prove it can work the other way.

ROY ESSANDOH, THE TELETEXT STRIKER

Wycombe manager Lawrie Sanchez had a chronic striker crisis in 2001 and, ten days before his third-tier club's FA Cup quarter-final at Leicester, he announced that he was desperate for a frontman. The story was picked up on Teletext and spotted by down-on-his-luck journeyman Roy Essandoh, a Northern Irish-Ghanaian, the only forward to get in touch with Sanchez. The following week, Essandoh came off the bench against the Foxes to score the late winner that sent Wycombe into the semi-finals for the first time in their history.

BRIAN MCDERMOTT'S iPAD

Just as so many managers have learned of their demises via text message or 24-hour sports news channels, one found out he had received a stay of execution via the internet. Leeds boss Brian McDermott was sacked by the club's potential new owners one Friday night, only to discover via his iPad on the Saturday that he was actually still the club's manager – but it was too late to turn up to work for that day's game against Huddersfield.

BEN FOSTER'S PENALTY SHOOT-OUT iPOD

The 2009 League Cup final between Manchester United and Spurs had gone to penalties and Reds goalkeeper Ben Foster could be seen on the pitch looking at a small device before the shoot-out started. What was this witchcraft? 'Just before the shoot-out I was looking at an iPod with goalkeeping coach Eric Steele and it contained images of Tottenham's players taking penalties,' explained Foster.

The players he watched included Jamie O'Hara, whose spot-kick Foster subsequently saved as United won the cup.

GOAL-LINE TECHNOLOGY

No more arguments, no more ghost goals, no more World Cup what ifs – the new technology has finally laid to rest all that 'was it or wasn't it?' over the line nonsense, which has to be a good thing. When Manchester City racked up their 100th goal of the 2013/14 season, it was only given by the Hawk-Eye system – proving that it actually worked.

ARSENAL v ARSENAL RESERVES, 16 SEPTEMBER 1937

On the surface, this doesn't sound like the most riveting of fixtures, certainly not one you would sit down in your living room with your mates to watch. Yet that's exactly what a few people would have done all those years ago, as this was the first ever live televised game – well, 15 minutes of it was broadcast by the BBC anyway. Without it, we wouldn't be able to enjoy Copa America, Bundesliga or any other global football match of our choice wherever we are in the world today.

EVERTON'S *FOOTBALL MANAGER* OBSESSION

We all love a bit of football simulation in our spare time, but the *Football Manager* craze is now way beyond a computer game, as proven by the deal Everton did with Sports Interactive, the company behind the smash hit. When David Moyes was manager he signed an agreement to have access to the game's database, putting him in touch with an estimated 370,000 players from 20,000 teams across the world.

BAKU'S *FOOTBALL MANAGER*

Staying with *Football Manager*, countless applicants for managerial positions have been turned down despite presenting their gaming experience on a CV, but one 21-year-old struck it lucky. Vugar Guloglan oglu Huseynzade was taken on by the Azerbaijani Premier League side FK Baku as an advisor on the back of his ten years' experience of playing *Football Manager*, and soon after he was placed in charge of the club's reserve team. So don't give up sending in those CVs just yet.

FOOTBALL'S MOST MISTAKEN IDENTITIES

Just like when I texted Paddy instead of my wife and ran into his irate missus, football has seen many beautiful, unfortunate and occasionally hilarious cases of mistaken identity. These are my favourites.

ALI DIA

Probably the king of all mistaken identities, Southampton manager Graeme Souness believed Ali Dia was a very good footballer – sadly, he was not. The Saints boss received a phone call in 1996 from someone claiming to be striking sensation George Weah, urging him to take a look at 'Senegal international Ali Dia'. With an injury crisis mounting, Souness fell for the ruse, and Dia joined up with the squad for a match against Leeds after just a day's training. Saints legend Matt Le Tissier takes up the story: 'It probably would never have been an issue if I hadn't pulled my thigh muscle halfway through the first half and had to come off. The manager... decided to replace me with Mr Dia... His performance was almost comical. He kind of took my place, but he didn't really have a position. He was just wandering everywhere. I don't think he realised what position he was supposed to be in... In the end he got himself subbed because he was that bad.'

Mr Dia then had the temerity to report to the club's physio the following day for treatment on an injury, before disappearing from Southampton for good.

KIERON GIBBS

The Arsenal full-back was minding his own business when his team-mate Alex Oxlade-Chamberlain thought he was the goalkeeper and dived full length to turn Eden Hazard's shot around a post in a 2014 match against Chelsea. Referee Andre Marriner promptly awarded a penalty and then, for reasons only he will know, showed Gibbs a red card. Everyone protested, Oxlade-Chamberlain even told the ref he was the culprit but it was to no avail. Marriner later admitted he was 'disappointed' with the decision.

THE WRONG DA SILVA

Chris Foy also suffered a touch of the Marriners during a League Cup tie between Manchester United and Barnsley – although with twins on the pitch, he had a bit of an excuse. After Rafael da Silva was penalised for a challenge on Barnsley's Jamal Campbell-Ryce, Foy duly booked his identical brother Fabio. Oops.

CHRIS HOY

Foy was also in the thick of the action when Spurs played Stoke in 2011. He incurred the wrath of many irate Tottenham fans for sending off Younes Kaboul and generally not giving them enough decisions for their liking. Some of the less intelligent fans took to Twitter to vent their frustrations and managed to send all their messages to British Olympic cycling legend Sir Chris Hoy instead.

With Chris ~~Foy~~ Hoy

Luckily, the knight saw the funny side of almost having the same name as the ref, tweeting: 'Just for the record 1) I don't need glasses and 2) I do not lead a double life as an English premier league ref. That's Chris Foy.'

BREDE HANGELAND

To complete the set of hapless officials, Belgian referee Paul Allaerts also did a Marriner but he at least had the good sense to make amends. Fulham were playing Roma in a Europa League tie when Stephen Kelly was ruled to have fouled John Arne Riise in the penalty area. Allaerts took swift action, awarding the Italians a spot-kick and sending off Brede Hangeland for no apparent reason. The ref's six fellow officials didn't come to his assistance but the players on the pitch certainly did, causing the Belgian to change his mind and switch the red card to Kelly.

DIXIE DEAN

You don't score 60 goals in a season without being able to mix it with your opponents and Everton legend Dixie Dean was no shrinking violet. When he was just 17, Dean was the victim of a terrible challenge by an Altrincham defender, who caused him to lose a testicle. Dean went through his career believing his assailant went by the name of Davy Parks, and was certain he'd met his nemesis in a Liverpool pub 17 years later. In a friendly gesture, the man sent a pint across the bar for Dean, but the fiery striker was having none of it and hit Parks, sending him to hospital.

Job done. Or so it seemed until Dean found out that the Altrincham player actually went by the name of Molyneux.

MICHAEL KEANE

Another tale of twin trouble saw England Under-21 manager Gareth Southgate having to change his starting line-up at the last minute. Someone at the FA had mistakenly registered Will Keane, instead of his brother Michael, to play. Unfortunately for Southgate, he hadn't even selected Will in his squad and was forced to take Michael out of the team when the cock-up was pointed out to him less than an hour before kick-off in a match against Wales.

KARL POWER

The serial prankster's greatest moment was arguably posing as a Manchester United player at Bayern Munich's Olympiastadion before a Champions League game.

Power disguised himself as a member of the TV crew to gain pitchside access but when the United team gathered for a photograph before kick-off, he removed his clothes to reveal a full United kit underneath and quickly joined the team shot, to the bemusement of several players.

TOGO

A fake player like Power is one thing, but a fake team is a different level of mistaken identity altogether. When Bahrain strolled to a 3-0 friendly win over Togo in 2010, their coach smelled a rat. Josef Hickersberger was surprised that the opposition hadn't been fit enough to play 90 minutes, and it soon became clear that was because the opposition were not, in fact, the Togo national team. They were imposters.

And this was soon confirmed by the Togo soccer federation president General Seyi Memene, who said: 'The players who took part in the friendly against Bahrain were completely fake. We have not sent any team of footballers to Bahrain.'

It remains unclear as to how this was even possible, with rumours of a fake agent organising the game. What is clear is that this has never happened before – apart from the jokers who posed as England at the 2010 World Cup.

JASON BENT

Another fake player who made it on to the pitch was Manchester City 'star' Jason Bent. The footballer, one of comedian Simon Brodkin's characters, appeared on the pitch dressed in full City training kit to warm up with his 'team-mates' before a 2013 Premier League match at Everton's Goodison Park. He performed a few stretches, shuttle runs and dodgy keepy-uppies while Joe Hart, Kolo Toure, David Silva and City coach David Platt wondered who on earth he was.

At roughly the same time, security officials were thinking the same thing and marched him off the pitch, where he was arrested. Bent eventually received a six-month conditional caution after a judge at North Liverpool Community Justice Centre agreed to drop charges. Outside court, Bent quipped: 'I want to thank the judge, who was sat on the bench but unfortunately didn't get a game.'

A year later, Bent donned an England World Cup suit and attempted to board the team plane on the Luton airport tarmac, only to be escorted away by security again.

MASAL BUGDUV

A few years ago, *The Times* included promising Moldovan teenage footballer Masal Bugduv as one of their Top 50 Rising Stars – unfortunately, he didn't actually exist.

The paper, and many websites, were the victims of a hoax by Irish pranksters who set up blogs about Bugduv, as well as a Wikipedia page which suggested that Arsenal were tracking the 16-year-old. The name chosen by the hoaxers was not dissimilar to '*M'asal Beag Dubh*', an old Gaelic tale about a man who tried to sell a lazy donkey. Did you see what they did there?

COMPUTER XI

Seeing as we spend most of our lives on social media these days, it's only fitting to close this chapter with a Computer XI:

Team Name: MotherBordeaux
Reserves: Printer Milan
Stadium: Comic Sans Siro
Training Ground: Byte Hart Lane

Management Team
Qwerty Vogts

First Team
Edwindows Van Der Sar
MSN Boyce (c)
Snes Brown
Abdoulaye Wi Faye
Jaap Spam
Atari Litmanen
Giovanni MS Dos Santos
Rory Delaptop
Peter Modemwingie
Marouane Chamacbook
Leroy Ctrl Alt DeLita

Subs
Martin Fulopy Disc
Jonathan Spectrum
Wii-sung Park
Dell Piero
Jan Vennegoor Of Hyperlink
Shift Key Kuqi

CLASSIC FOOTBALL INJURIES

Anyone who has played football, at any level, will have picked up some sort of injury. At one end you've got the overweight father who tears his groin while trying to show he 'still has it' at a family barbecue and, at the other, the cruciate ligament tear that wrecks the dreams and, in some cases, careers of professionals.

Our obsession with footballers' pain has accelerated with the need to fill 24-hour news channels. Before the 2002 World Cup in Japan and South Korea 'metatarsals' sounded like something that attacked the Starship Enterprise! 'We're under attack... it's the Klingons in league with the Metatarsals.'

Now we all seem to know our medulla oblongata from our gastrocnemius and we could make a long list of players whose major tournament build-up has been shattered by the mighty metatarsal. We shall go on to discuss other injuries to players later in the chapter, but I would briefly like to detail three medical issues that have had the greatest effect on me – none of which involves a little bone in the foot.

There are many of you reading this who will feel that your true footballing promise was curtailed by an injury. In my early years I was a decent player based largely on the fact that I was the kid who was over 6ft at the age of five (slight exaggeration). My opposition, up until the age of about 12, thought I was a giant. In my mid-teens I discovered I was in fact distinctly average but my full potential was never realised due to the first of five knee dislocations at the age of 16. I went from being able to run 100m in 12 seconds dead to a 16-second, last-on-sports-day type.

I was waddling down the wing and, as I planted my right leg, the left-back went over the top of the ball and the next thing I knew I was on my way to hospital with my kneecap somewhere near the middle of my right shin. It has popped out four times since – three of those were football related... the other involved running away from a sheep!

The most comical injury I had witnessed happened in the presence of the great Emilio Butragueno in the President's Suite at the Bernabeu in Madrid. These interviews normally last about 20 to 30 minutes, so it's important that everyone is in a comfortable position for the duration. For some reason – still unknown – our locally hired cameraman decided to film the entire interview in a position that can only be described as a 'power crouch'.

We were all concerned that he couldn't maintain it for more than a minute but in fairness he lasted a full seven before collapsing in a cramp-filled pile on the floor. The sweat was pouring off his head as he gripped his quads thinking he would never see them again. Butragueno was very polite and went to make a phone call for ten minutes. I used the time to test the flush on the president's toilet. Impressive.

I'm sorry to say that cramp rears its ugly head here too. Do you remember the 'prawn sandwich' quote from Roy Keane? It came after a 1-0 win over Dynamo Kiev in the Champions League in November 2000. I was in the Old Trafford tunnel that night, in a media huddle waiting for players to pass comment on the game. There were about 25 of us and we'd been told by the press officer that Roy would stop. The commentator Steve Bower – then at MUTV – had his position at the front of the barriers and the rest of us all filtered in behind. I had got there a little later than normal so was about three rows back and had to extend my arm to its full capacity and then rest my microphone on Steve's head. When Keane rounded the corner you could tell he had that little glint in his eye – something was coming.

As I remember it, Steve asked a question about some of the fans criticising the performance of Mikael Silvestre and that was all the invitation the Manchester United captain needed. 'Away from home our fans are fantastic, I'd call them the hardcore fans. But at home they have a few drinks and probably the prawn sandwiches, and they don't realise what's going on out on the pitch. I don't think some of the people who come to Old Trafford can spell "football", never mind understand it.'

It was a headline writer's dream and an answer that flung 'prawn sandwiches' into the football lexicon. Sadly, I have rather painful memories of the interview because for the full duration of it my right arm was stretched out far beyond its normal parameters. As Keane started speaking the masses gathered and there was all sorts of jostling going on. I lost my resting point on the top of Bower's noggin and as Keane continued to speak I could feel an almost unbearable burn in my right shoulder.

My dad always says it's impossible to hold a pint of water with an outstretched arm for longer than seven minutes. I've never tried it but I challenge anyone to hold a microphone out, standing on your tiptoes, with your head wedged between a sweaty man's back and a TV camera for ten. I have since had surgery on the right shoulder but I told the doctor it was a chronic sports injury and nothing to do with prawns.

Roy Keane's Greatest Hits

The prawn sandwich rant was just the tip of the iceberg when it comes to the fearsome Irishman's verbal lashings. Here are my favourite Keane utterances, not all of which I witnessed at such close quarters – luckily for my shoulder.

On Playing Football
'Aggression is what I do. I go to war. You don't contest football matches in a reasonable state of mind.'

On Life Off the Pitch
'The amount of fights I've had in Cork would probably be another book. I mean, people go on about my problems off the field, but they don't even know the half of it.'

On the Alf-Inge Haaland Tackle
'I'd waited long enough. I f*****g hit him hard. The ball was there (I think). Take that you c***. And don't ever stand over me again sneering about fake injuries. And tell your pal [David] Wetherall there's some for him as well. I didn't wait for Mr Elleray to show the red card. I turned and walked to the dressing room. My attitude is an eye for an eye.'

On Loyalty
'I remember having conversations with [Ferguson] about loyalty. In my opinion he doesn't know the meaning of the word.'

On Rio Ferdinand
'Just because you are paid a hundred and twenty thousand pounds a week and play well for twenty minutes against Tottenham, you think you are a superstar.'

On Mick McCarthy

'Mick, you're a liar... you're a f*****g w****r. I didn't rate you as a player, I don't rate you as a manager, and I don't rate you as a person. You're a f*****g w****r and you can stick your World Cup up your a**e. The only reason I have any dealings with you is that somehow you are the manager of my country! You can stick it up your b******s.'

On FIFA Vice-President Jack Warner

'Although [Warner's] working for Trinidad and Tobago he's writing under FIFA letterheads, trying to impress everybody. Forget all this talk about directors of football – if he's vice-president of FIFA, God help everybody.'

On Wives Scuppering Transfer Deals

'These so-called big stars are people we are supposed to be looking up to. Well, they are weak and soft. If they don't want to come because their wife wants to go shopping in London, it's a sad state of affairs. I can understand the attraction of people wanting to go to London – if you are talking about Arsenal, Chelsea or Tottenham. If people want to go somewhere else to another football club then fair enough, as long as it is for a footballing reason. But there are players going to clubs in London simply because it is London.'

On Clive Clarke's On-pitch Heart Attack

'On a night we got beaten in the cup by Luton, the staff came in and said, "Clive Clarke has had a heart attack at Leicester." I said, "Is he OK? I'm shocked they found one, you could never tell by the way he plays."'

On Taking a Brian Clough Punch

'Cloughie was dead right, absolutely. It was the best thing he ever did for me. It's good to get angry. It's an emotion and part of the game. It's good to go a bit mad but I don't throw teacups around. That's not my style – I'd rather throw punches.'

On Below-par TV Pundits

'Will those on telly yesterday be remembered for what they've achieved? None whatsoever. I wouldn't trust them to walk my dog. There are ex-players and ex-referees being given air-time who I wouldn't listen to in a pub.'

FOOTBALLERS
AND TOILETS

I had a wonderful time in the Bernabeu's presidential loo, time enough to get me thinking about a series of footballing incidents revolving around calls of nature. This is probably not one to read with your dinner.

JENS LEHMANN

The former Arsenal goalkeeper was playing for Stuttgart in a European tie when he felt he had to go, so he did the equivalent of a drunk finding an alley, and went behind an advertising hoarding near his goal. Fortunately for all concerned, it was a number one.

FABIEN BARTHEZ

What is it with urinating goalkeepers? The Frenchman took full advantage of 60,000 eyes on his Marseille side attacking Inter Milan's goal in a 2004 UEFA Cup tie by watering his penalty area at the other end while nobody was looking.

BARRY FRY

The larger-than-life former Birmingham manager took matters into his own hands when the Blues were suffering a terrible run of form. He'd heard there was a curse on St Andrews so decided to take on the evil spirit by weeing on all four corners of the pitch. It didn't work and it wasn't long before Barry was on his way.

ROBBIE SAVAGE

There are two versions of this story, but both of them involve the former Leicester midfielder doing a number two in referee Graham Poll's changing-room loo. If you don't want to know any more, look away now. Before the Foxes played Villa at Filbert Street, Savage was desperate for the loo so ran into the referee's room and used his cubicle, before wiping his hands on the lapels of the referees' assessor's jacket. That was Poll's version.

Robbie claimed in his autobiography that both loos in the home dressing room were busy and, with a bad case of the runs due to some antibiotics and only ten minutes to kick-off, he had no choice – wiping his hands on the assessor's jacket was a joke which everyone laughed at.

In any event, Savage was fined £10,000 by the FA for improper conduct.

CRYSTAL PALACE

When Ian Holloway's Palace side arrived at Brighton for the second leg of their 2013 Championship play-off semi-final, they were shocked to discover excrement smeared all over the toilet and shower area of the away dressing room. Nobody owned up to the prank, but it clearly riled the visitors who went on to win the match 2-0. Brighton apologised, but the damage had been done.

A CHILEAN DOG

England were playing Brazil in the 1962 World Cup when a dog invaded the pitch, managing to evade all attempts to catch it, until England striker Jimmy Greaves caught up with the mutt and picked it up. His reward for his intervention was a healthy helping of the dog's urine all over his England kit.

GARY LINEKER

In the opening game of the 1990 World Cup against Ireland, the national icon was suffering with a stomach bug but soldiered on. In an interview on Radio 5 Live, Lineker described what happened during the second half when he stretched into a tackle. 'The ball went down the left-hand side. I did try to tackle someone. I stretched and then I "relaxed myself". I was very fortunate it rained that night and I could do something about it. It was messy, it just came out, it happened. It was the most horrendous experience of my life. But I tell you I never found so much space in a game than I did that night after that happened.'

LIAM RIDGEWELL

The West Brom player hit the headlines for the wrong reasons in 2012 when a photograph emerged showing him squatting over a toilet and wiping his behind with a £20 note, as bundles more £20 notes lay on the floor. Oops. The picture had only been intended as a wind-up on a friend of Ridgewell's who had just lost a bet with the defender but, as is always the way nowadays, it ended up in the wrong hands and the player was forced to apologise.

LOICK PIRES

During a Conference South clash between Welling and Woking, the home side's striker Loick Pires was desperate for the loo. But instead of doing a subtle Lehmann or Barthez-style pee, he leapt on to the terraces and went into one of the fans' loos. About 40 seconds later, he returned to the pitch and was booked by the referee for leaving and/or entering the field of play without permission.

GLEN JOHNSON

Back in 2007, the England right-back was nicked for trying to switch a more expensive toilet seat in a Dartford B&Q into a cheaper box – and hiding some bath taps in a sink at the checkout. Along with his accomplice, Millwall striker Ben May, he was handed an £80 on-the-spot fine for theft.

JASON PUNCHEON

The Southampton man had to leave the field to answer a call of nature during a Premier League game against Everton. When he sheepishly returned to the pitch a couple of minutes later, he was greeted by away fans chanting, to the tune of 'Sloop John B' (of course! I have slighty adjusted the words for our younger readers):

He went for a poo
He went for a poo
Jason Puncheon
He went for a poo

But that wasn't the end of the japes as, moments later, the Saints fans responded with the following to the same tune:

He poos when he wants
He poos when he wants
Jason Puncheon
He poos when he wants

FERGIE

The Manchester United manager used a call of nature to escape an illegal driving charge in 1999, after he was caught using the hard shoulder on a heavily congested motorway. Sir Alex claimed he was suffering with severe diarrhoea on the M602 and had no choice but to drive in the emergency lane. Although police followed him and cautioned him on the spot, he was found not guilty when he fully explained himself in court.

Football's Most Injured Players

It's tough for me to admit but with five knee dislocations, I may be a tad delicate. However, that's nothing compared to these pros who have spent way more time in the physio's room than the changing room. Poor lads.

Kieron Dyer

Before he joined West Ham in 2007, Dyer had done quite well to play more than 300 games for Ipswich, Newcastle and England. But that was relative to what was to come next as the midfielder only managed 25 starts during the next six years at the Hammers, Ipswich (again), QPR and Middlesbrough. Injuries included a 17-month lay-off for a double leg-break and a foot ligament problem, which meant he only played seven minutes of the 2011/12 season. He called it a day in 2013.

Darren 'Sicknote' Anderton

The nickname says it all, but Anderton actually played a little more than Jamie Redknapp – more about him in a moment. Anderton's nadir occurred between 1995 and 1998 at Spurs, where he made only 43 appearances due to a combination of hernia, knee and groin problems. The following year, Achilles surgery ruled him out for another three months.

Jamie Redknapp

A constant battle against knee injuries saw Redknapp's career curtailed at the age of just 31. In terms of averages he played fewer games per season than Anderton although he did manage 250 for Liverpool over ten years. A move to Spurs saw his average plummet, with only 48 league games in two and a half seasons, before an attempt to help his old man at relegation-bound Southampton also ended in injury and his subsequent retirement.

Abou Diaby

Arsenal's midfield tough guy has never really been available for the Gunners, which may explain why they struggled in that area in his first eight years at the club. Only 123 appearances in that time due to a series of minor injuries and a major cruciate knee problem meant the sight of Diaby in an Arsenal shirt was as rare as Arsene Wenger seeing any controversial incident involving anyone on his team... ever!

Stuart Holden

The Bolton midfielder has not enjoyed much luck since his move to the North-west from Houston in 2010. He was ruled out for six months after a clash with Manchester United's Jonny Evans left him with a serious knee injury. Further cartilage damage was discovered at the time of his comeback, meaning another six months out, and he followed that up with a cruciate ligament rupture while on international duty with the USA. Holden's comeback from that setback lasted just 20 minutes before the knee problem resurfaced and he faced another lengthy spell on the sidelines. In three years, he made just 28 league appearances for the Trotters. Ouch.

Owen Hargreaves

After being named England's best player at the 2006 World Cup, the future seemed to be bright for the defensive midfielder. But that proved to be the highlight as a series of knee injuries (left and right) and a broken leg more or less ruined his career, although he did find time to help Manchester United win the Champions League against Chelsea in 2008. Hargreaves made his first start for United for more than two years in 2010, but his hamstring gave way after just six minutes. After 27 appearances in four years at United, he joined Manchester City in 2011, but made only four appearances for them before hanging up his boots, aged 31.

Jonathan Woodgate

The already injury-prone former Leeds and Newcastle defender joined Real Madrid for a whopping £13.4 million in 2004 but was immediately ruled out for a year through injury. He eventually made a spectacular debut in September 2005 against Athletic Bilbao, when he scored an own goal and was sent off. He only managed nine La Liga appearances for the Spanish club before returning to England on loan at Middlesbrough and then joining Spurs. Injury struck again there when a groin problem ruled him out for 14 months between 2009 and 2011, and his comeback from that setback, against AC Milan in the Champions League, ended with an abductor muscle injury, which was the last time he played for the White Hart Lane club. He soldiered on and eventually went back to Middlesbrough, where he hasn't thrown in the towel. Yet.

Michael Owen

Until 2006, Owen's career was stellar, but a serious knee injury while playing for England in the World Cup changed everything, robbing the striker of his fitness and pace forever. He managed just 71 league games for Newcastle over the next four years, before making 31 similar appearances for Manchester United for the three seasons after that, mainly being used as a squad player due to a lack of form and fitness. A brief spell at Stoke was followed by retirement – but he'll always have that goal against Argentina.

THE ORIGINS OF FOOTBALL'S MOST PECULIAR LEXICON

Thanks to my 'hilarious' anecdote we now know the origins of the prawn sandwich bit of football idiom. But what of those other everyday phrases we hear in the football world – from whence do they originate? Let's find out.

PARKING THE BUS

Now commonly used to describe a team's ultra-defensive tactics, this first entered the football lexicon back in 2004, when Chelsea boss Jose Mourinho was frustrated by a Spurs side that came to Stamford Bridge to defend and claimed a point in a dour 0-0 draw. 'Tottenham might as well have put the team bus in front of their goal,' he said after the match.

SQUEAKY-BUM TIME

From round about March onwards, this phrase is used to describe any tight climax to a league season and was first used by Sir Alex Ferguson to describe the thrilling finale to the 2002/03 campaign, when United and Arsenal went head-to-head. 'It's getting tickly now – squeaky-bum time, I call it,' he said.

NOISY NEIGHBOURS

The phrase that is starting to be used across football to describe a rival team was also coined by Ferguson, when talking about Manchester City's rise to prominence. 'Sometimes you have a noisy neighbour,' he said. 'You cannot do anything about that. They will always be noisy. You just have to get on with your life, put your television on and turn it up a bit louder.'

THE HAIRDRYER

Another Fergie phrase, although it was Mark Hughes who started this one – it means to give someone a right good verbal rollicking. Hughes was describing how Ferguson used to reprimand him or his team-mates, saying: 'He would stand nose-to-nose with you and just shout and bawl, and you would end up with your hair behind your head.'

THE FALSE NINE

This is the term modern football has coined for the fairly old practice of deploying a centre-forward in a very deep position, closer to midfield. The number nine was traditionally the centre-forward or striker's number, so when that player drops much deeper, he's known as a false nine. Austrian and Hungarian teams in the 1930s and 1950s respectively were the first to use the tactic, but it's been employed regularly by Spain, Barcelona and many other sides in recent years. Who first called it a false nine? No idea, but for the sake of argument let's say it was Tony Yeboah's mum.

HANDBAGS

This phrase is used to describe any physical altercation on a pitch between two or more players that doesn't actually end in a proper fight – in other words, pretty much every single physical altercation on a football pitch. It was first used as a longer phrase by manager and TV pundit Ron Atkinson in the 1980s. He would say, 'That was handbags at dawn' or 'handbags at ten paces', to describe a ruckus in a demeaning way using old English duelling terminology. That quickly became shortened to just 'handbags' and here we are.

EARLY DOORS

Now universally known as a way of describing something that happened in the early stages of a football match, this was another Big Ron creation which he more or less forced into the football lexicon whether anyone liked it or not by repeatedly using it every time he was on air. Nobody has any idea why the 'doors' bit is actually necessary but, despite the absurdity, no one ever questions it.

FERGIE TIME

Another way of saying excessive time added on by a referee at the end of a match, given Manchester United's habit of scoring crucial late goals. The phrase was coined by *Guardian* reporter Jeremy Alexander in a 1998 match report of a United defeat at Sheffield Wednesday: 'Shortly after, the Wednesday bench held up No. 11 and No. 19, suggesting 11 minutes of injury-time and 19 of Fergie-time, that special allowance when United are behind.'

STONEWALL PENALTY

When I was growing up, it was either a penalty or it wasn't. These days, however, if it's a penalty, it's a 'stonewall' one, and if it isn't, well, it isn't. The phrase has become overused thanks to the likes of Paul Merson and other *Soccer Saturday* regulars who called every incident in the box a stonewall penalty. Managers soon picked up on it, and the beautiful game had some ugly new language. Just to clarify, the three possible decisions when there is a foul in the box:

1. No penalty
2. Penalty
3. Stonewall penalty

ILLNESS XI

There is really only one way to go at the end of this chapter. Ladies and gentlemen, I present your Illness XI...

Team Name: Bed Panathinaikos
Reserves: Plaster Of Paris St Germain
Stadium: GalPharmacy
Training Ground: Operating Theatre Of Dreams

Chairman
Pile Quinn

Management Team
ChrisPowell Movement
Lawrie McEnema
Louis Van Gaalitosis
Tord Drip

First Team

Headwound Van Der Scar	Mortem Gamst Medicine
Radek Gurney	Steven Pie-naar
HepaTitus Bramble	Pie-naar Pie-naar
Papa BUPA Preop	Zlatan IntravenousDrip
NHEssien (c)	Djibril CisseSection
X-Ray Parlour	Marouane FellA&E

Subs
Alan Scrubs

Diego MarrowDonor	Stress FractureGas
Robin Van Nursie	Splint Dempsey

ACKNOWLEDGEMENTS

I have been reliably informed by the lovely publishing people at Simon & Schuster that this is an essential part of any book. I will start by thanking Ian Marshall and everyone at S&S for thinking that this was a worthy venture to embark upon.

Thanks also to Jonny McWilliams and Jonathan Conway for their encouragement and backside-kicking, and Gershon Portnoi (yes, that is his actual name) for being brilliant and funny and having excellent hair.

A significant 'ta' to my parents for teaching me the importance of communication and to John Pickford – my first broadcasting boss – for honing those skills and showing me how to best use them when people were actually listening.

There are loads of people I have worked and travelled with on various jobs over the years, who have been great company and creative genii – far too many for me to note down here. You know who you are, and if you're not sure, it's probably not you.

Thanks to the woman who turned me down for teacher training – a decision that forced me to sign up for a post-graduate course in broadcast journalism – and big love to you lot for all your contributions to Tuesday Team News and for making me spit out various beverages with your puns and suggestions.

Thanks to the big bloke who didn't 'punch my head in' on a family holiday in Scotland in the early 1990s. His promise to 'follow me home' and 'end me' turned out to be merely empty threats which – if followed through – would have made writing this a little more difficult.

Big love to the magnificent Lady Susie of Dent, who was kind enough to pen the foreword to this tome. She is brilliant on TV and remains genuine, kind and effortlessly lovely off it.

Thanks to all the good friends who have helped and encouraged me over the years, particularly Ed Hoyland, who I persuaded to pretend to be me once against his better judgement. Although his caution was correct, it did open the door to professional employment.

Most importantly of all, my heartfelt thanks go to my wife and kids who are all wonderful and long-suffering, and to God (and not in an American popstar way), without whom I am sure a word of this would never have been written.

Oh, and thanks to Des Lynam for answering my letter when I was 11 and making me think a career in all this sort of stuff was actually possible.

BIBLIOGRAPHY

In the course of researching this book, the following resources were used:

45football.com
bbc.co.uk
bleacherreport.com
dailymail.co.uk
dailyrecord.co.uk
dailystar.co.uk
express.co.uk
football365.com
footballburp.com
fourfourtwo.com
goal.com
independent.co.uk

mirror.co.uk
skysports.com
soccerbase.com
talksport.com
telegraph.co.uk
thefa.com
theguardian.com
thesun.co.uk
thetimes.co.uk
twitter.com
uk.eurosport.yahoo.com
What You See Is What You

Get: My Autobiography,
Alan Sugar (Macmillan,
2010)
*Who Are Ya? The
talkSPORT Book of
Football's Best Ever
Chants*, Gershon Portnoi
(Simon & Schuster,
2011)
whoateallthepies.tv
youtube.com

CREDITS